Up, Down, Move Around
Math and Literacy
Active Learning for Preschoolers

by Deborah Kayton Michals

Dedication

This book is dedicated to the inspirational examples and memories of my mother, Marjorie Kayton—a creative and passionately committed preschool music teacher; and my grandmother, Lillian Klempner—a dedicated teacher of literacy and math.

Acknowledgements

I express my grateful appreciation in particular to Megan Bascom for her essential work in the research, organization, and writing of these books; to Angessa Hughmanick and Kimberly Lantz for their contributions; to Phyllis Lyons, director of Selma Maisel Preschool, for her support and viewpoint; and to Florence Phillips, Don Adams, Amy Bilden, Leslie Dobryn, Debbi Korn, and Dale Walkonen, who contributed to literacy or art materials. Thanks very much to my editor, Stephanie Roselli, and to Clarissa Willis and the Gryphon House team for their work, and to Kathy Charner and Melinda Scrivner for their encouragement. Thanks to Alan Lopatin, lobbyist on behalf of young children and others who can't advocate for themselves, whose work brought these books into existence. And thanks to my husband, Jonathan Michals, and my children, Ali, Ben, and Katie, whose contributions inspire me daily.

Up, Down, Move Around
Math and Literacy

Active Learning for Preschoolers

Deborah Michals

Gryphon House

Lewisville, NC

Copyright

©2013 Deborah Kayton Michals

Published by Gryphon House, Inc.
P. O. Box 10, Lewisville, NC 27023
800.638.0928; 877.638.7576 (fax)

Visit us on the web at www.gryphonhouse.com.

Library of Congress Cataloging-in-Publication Data

Michals, Deborah Kayton.
 Up, down, move around--math and Literacy : active learning for preschoolers / by Deborah Kayton Michals.
    pages cm.
 Includes bibliographical references and index.
 ISBN 978-0-87659-417-9 (pbk.)
1. Mathematics and physical education. 2. Mathematics--Study and teaching (Preschool)--Activity programs. 3. Active learning. 4. Early childhood education. I. Title. II. Title: Math and literacy.
 QA20.P49M53 2013
 372.7'044--dc23
                              2012041679

Bulk Purchase

Gryphon House books are available for special premiums and sales promotions as well as for fund-raising use. Special editions or book excerpts also can be created to specifications. For details, contact the Director of Marketing at Gryphon House.

Disclaimer

Gryphon House, Inc. cannot be held responsible for damage, mishap, or injury incurred during the use of or because of activities in this book. Appropriate and reasonable caution and adult supervision of children involved in activities and corresponding to the age and capability of each child involved is recommended at all times. Do not leave children unattended at any time. Observe safety and caution at all times.

Table of Contents

Foreword

by Rae Pica

I have dedicated my life's work to the belief that movement is one of the most important vehicles through which young children learn. Deborah Kayton Michals's *Up, Down, Move Around–Math and Literacy: Active Learning for Preschoolers* makes a significant contribution to helping educators understand this essential philosophy of teaching and learning and to helping teachers make movement a central part of the learning process.

Research demonstrates that movement is the young child's preferred mode of learning and that children learn best through active involvement. The more senses that a child uses in the learning process, the more information that child retains.

Up, Down, Move Around–Math and Literacy: Active Learning for Preschoolers offers early childhood professionals the opportunity to tap into that connection between movement and learning. With its dozens and dozens of activities, all with comprehensive, easy-to-follow instructions and detailed examples, users of this book will be able to make literacy and math come alive for children.

As they demonstrate actions from the beginning, middle, and end of a favorite story, children begin to understand story structure. When they clap on the rhythm of a rhyme, they are not only learning to recognize rhymes but also are being well prepared to internalize the rhythm that is essential to reading and writing. When children create action puzzles, they learn about pattern sequencing. When they take on geometric shapes with their bodies, they imprint the information, on the body and in the mind. All of these activities allow children to hear, see, and feel the lessons, ensuring they will make the intended impression—an impression that lasts!

Deborah's experience working with preschoolers in movement education and training teachers to use physical activity for learning makes her uniquely qualified to bring these lessons and activities to early childhood professionals.

Like me, she is puzzled by the concept of children simply sitting and listening to a book being read, and by the idea that children would not have the opportunity to experience concepts in the way that is most effective for them. Her intention with *Up, Down, Move Around—Math and Literacy: Active Learning for Preschoolers* is to remove the excuses that prevent children from learning through physical participation. I believe she's succeeded. Deborah's goal is to have every teacher declare, "Yes, I can do this in my classroom!" I say, "Brava, and amen to that!"

Introduction

Up, Down, Move Around—Math and Literacy: Active Learning for Preschoolers provides the tools to help you connect children's physical and cognitive development. Active play provides the most effective learning for preschoolers, giving you wonderful opportunities to influence children's learning in both hemispheres of the brain. Active learning sharpens auditory discrimination and multiple-intelligence learning as children listen to and process information, translating that information into physical activity. A child's attention becomes more focused during physical activity, and a great learning opportunity exists at this peak of focus.

Preschool children need to move. Physical activity is a pathway to cognitive learning for this age group. Research supports this connection between movement and physical, cognitive, social, and emotional development. In her book *Smart Moves,* Carla Hannaford states that movement integrates and anchors new information and that moving while learning increases learning. In "From Cartwheels to Caterpillars: Children's Need to Move Indoors and Out," Anita Olds says that connecting literacy concepts with physical experience imbeds the concepts and hardwires the associated synaptic relationships.

Use the activities in *Up, Down, Move Around—Math and Literacy: Active Learning for Preschoolers* to support and enhance the learning that you are already providing for the children in your classroom:

How to Use the Activities

The activities are flexible and easy to incorporate into your classroom routine:

- Everything you need is already in your classroom! No special materials, props, or extra space are required.
- Exercises can be done as 5- to 10-minute enrichment activities with your regular curriculum lesson
- Activities can be extended from 10 to 20 minutes to use as self-contained lessons

Letter recognitions	Number sense
Letter sounds	Number recognition
Syllables	Counting
Words	Patterns
Poetry	Sequence
Rhyming	Grouping and
Rhythm	sets
Story structure	Computation
Prediction	Geometric
One-to-one	shapes
correspondence	

- Exercises can be stacked, in groups of two to five, for up to an hour's worth of physical activity
- Use these exercises toward the 60 minutes of structured physical activity recommended for preschoolers in national guidelines and complement standard physical fitness games and exercises.*
- Use the activities with large and small groups, in circle time, and as transitions. Small-group time allows for more particularized attention to the individual child, while whole-group exercises benefit from the high energy level and multiple shapes and suggestions of a larger group.

There are many ways to do an activity correctly, and creative thinking and problem solving become the tools to be celebrated.

The activities physicalize the structures of reading and math, making them real, accessible, and understandable to young children. Reading exercises address letter recognition, words and vocabulary building, syllables, story structure, poetry, and rhymes. Math exercises teach specific learning concepts in number sense, one-to-one correspondence, counting, constructing sets, operations, geometric shapes, patterns and seriation, prediction, and spatial relationships.

Maximize your classroom time by integrating physical activity into multiple learning contexts. Active exercises gather the power of what children already know well—the strength, knowledge, and point of view of the world they understand through their bodies—and turn it toward classroom learning. To preschoolers, the most real and concrete concepts are physical; if learning is connected directly to the physical actions they already know, the learning will be more complete and lasting.

Up, Down, Move Around–Math and Literacy: Active Learning for Preschoolers provides the tools to help you develop gross and fine motor skills through fun, noncompetitive activities.

- Encourage children to explore their physical strengths and abilities.
- Create an atmosphere in which all ability levels are respected and accepted.
- Reach children who do not respond well to more sedentary activities or quiet learning.
- If there are children in your class who have special needs, use the activities to highlight positive aspects of the way they learn.
- Reach English language learners by helping them associate concepts with words before they actually know the vocabulary.

The creativity and open-ended responses invited through the exercises allow for and encourage this flexibility in your teaching.

I started out as a young teacher and dancer, teaching movement education in motor-skill development, creative thinking, self-confidence, and problem solving. As I taught, directed programs, and trained others over the course of more than 25 years, I saw that it was possible to use these methods to teach essential materials from the rest of the preschool day—pairing literacy and math skills with action for a powerful teaching tool. My experience integrating these aspects of action and learning inspired me to incorporate fitness, body awareness, and obesity prevention into a total-child approach. Then, First Lady Michelle Obama's 2009 "Let's Move" public-awareness campaign motivated this user-friendly guide to incorporate children's movements in developing their cognitive abilities.

The responsibility of the child for his or her body, if introduced early in ways children understand, can begin to be established with healthy patterns. The body is a child's first playground, and by connecting it clearly to the learning process, it can remain so in a world in which technology competes for their attention. By building action learning into the educational day, physicality and health become intertwined with and not separate from activities children want to do.

Up, Down, Move Around–Math and Literacy: Active Learning for Preschoolers presents solutions to the problem of fitting enough physical activity into your school day. Enjoy participating with the children in the activities in this book, moving the children and yourself with productive action throughout the day!

*National Association for Sports and Physical Education. 2009. *Active Start: A Statement of Physical Activity Guidelines for Children from Birth to Age 5*, 2nd edition. Reston, VA: NASPE.

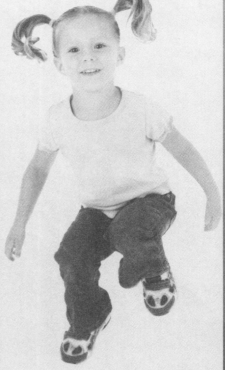

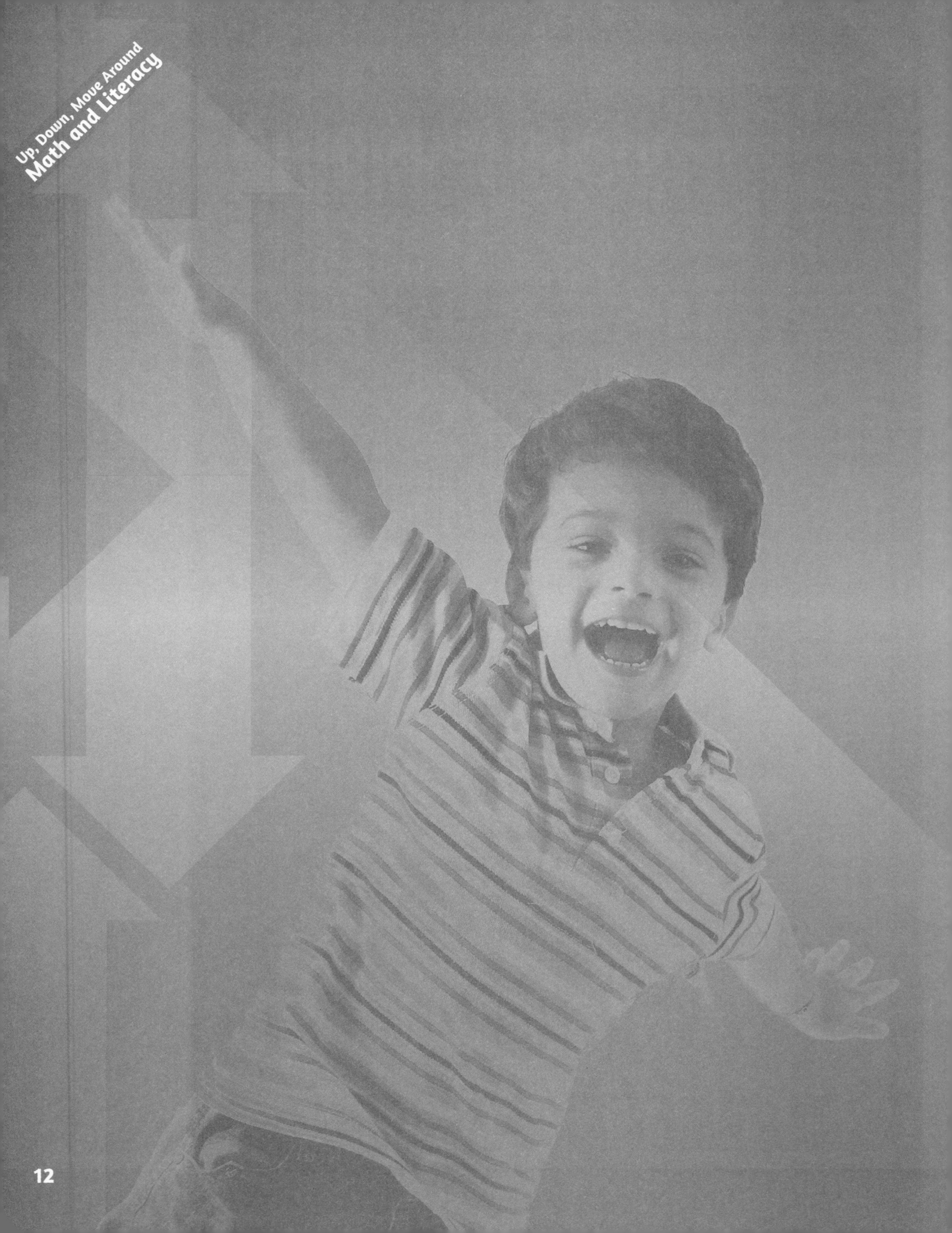

Move to Read

These literacy activities place children at the center of learning. Through physical connection, children can develop their understanding of letters, words, and story structure, suggesting an understanding of the power of children's own imaginations, intelligence, and movement capabilities. Taken together, these elements promote a child's ownership of the learning activities.

Letter Shapes

Reinforce learning the shapes of the letters in the alphabet.

How to Do It

1. Ask the children to sit in a circle or at a table. Show a picture of the letter they are learning—for example, the letter *A*. Ask them to draw it in the air and on the floor with their index fingers. Ask questions such as, "What does this letter *A* look like? I see a point at the top, like a triangle."

2. Encourage them to stand and make the letter with their bodies. If they are not sure how to do this, offer hints: "Can you make yourself into a pointy top? Make a point with your hands over your heads. Put your feet apart on the ground, just like that *A*. Now I see a line through the middle. Your head can be the line. I see those letter *A*s!"

3. Repeat this a couple of times. If the children have learned other letters, ask them to make those shapes with their bodies. For example, *B* can be made with the arms as two little circles pointing in and touching the belly.

My Name Is

Help children recognize the first letters of their names by associating an action that starts with the same letter.

How to Do It

1. Ask the children to stand in a circle. Let each child take a turn standing in the middle of the circle.

2. Say the name of that child and the first letter of her name—for example, "Danita! Danita starts with *D*."

3. Attach an action word that starts with the same letter as the child's name. You can pick out the action or help the child pick it out—for example, "Danita likes to dance."

4. Then chant, using the letter and each child's name in turn. Encourage the children to chant the rap with you:

   Danita, it's your turn.
   Danita likes to dance.
   D, D, D, D, D, D, D (Danita gets up and dances)
   My name is Danita
   And I like to play.
   I like to dance (Danita dances)
   And I like to say, "Hey!" (Danita waves hello and the children wave back to her)
   I like to dance and dance all day (Danita dances)
   I like to dance, and this is the way!
   Dance with Danita; dance and say, "Hey!" (Children get ready)
   D, D, D, D, D, D, D (Children all join in)
   Now everyone dance with Danita
   D, D, D, D, D, D, D,
   Dance and say, "Hooray!"

An Alphabet of Actions

A—act
B—bounce
C—catch or crawl
Cl—climb or clap
Ch—chase or cheer
D—dance
E—exercise
F—fall or frog jump
G—go
H—hop
I—imitate
J—jump
K—kick
L—laugh
M—move
N—noodle
O—go over
P—prance
Q—go quickly
R—run
S—skip or slide
Sh—shake or shimmy
T—twirl or twist or turn
U—go under
V—visit
W—wiggle
X—make *X*s (jumping jack)
Y—yoyo
Z—zigzag

A Is for Animal!

This is a fun call-and-response activity to reinforce learning the alphabet. Feel free to substitute any animal names that fit with your students' interests.

How to Do It

Ask the children to sit in a circle. Bounce and tap knees to the rhythm as you do the following alphabet chant:

A, B, C, and *D,* okay.
A is for alligator.
B is for bear.
C is for cat,
and
D is for dog.
E, F, G, and *H,* okay.
E is for elephant.
F is for fish.
G is for gorilla,
and *H* is for hen.
I, J, K, and *L,* okay.
I is for iguana.

J is for jaguar.
K is for kangaroo,
and *L* is for lion.
M, N, O, and *P,* okay.
M is for monkey.
N is for nest.
O is for ostrich,
and *P* is for penguin.
Q, R, S, and *T,* okay.
Q is for quail.
R is for rooster.
S is for snake,
and *T* is for tiger.

U, V, W, and *X,* okay.
U is for unicorn.*
V is for viper.
W is for whale,
and *X* is for x-ray fish.
Y and *Z,* okay!
Y is for yak, and
Z is for zebra!

*Of course, a unicorn is not a real animal, but if you put it in, children will have fun telling you!

ABC Rap

This is an upbeat twist on that old standby, "The Alphabet Song."

How to Do It

1. Ask the children stand up, and begin a side-to-side stepping and clapping action.
2. Chant the following:
   A-B-C-D-E-F-G (step, clap, step, clap, step, clap, step, clap)
   H-I-J-K-L-M-N (step, clap, step, clap, step, clap, step, clap)
   O-P-Q (step, clap, step, clap)
   R-S-T (step, clap, step, clap)
   U-V-W-X-Y-Z! (step, clap, step, clap, step, clap)
3. Slow down the rhythm a bit, and add a little wiggle in between the steps and claps.

Alphabet Books

Pairing movements with specific letters of the alphabet can help children remember their letters.

How to Do It

1. Choose a book to read to the children that has the alphabet as its theme, such as *My Shimmery Alphabet Book* by Salina Yoon.
2. As you read, stop at each letter to make an action sequence that acts out the picture in the book for that letter. For example, in *My Shimmery Alphabet,* the picture for the letter *A* is an ape. Encourage the children to write the letter *A* in the air, to make an *A* with their bodies, and to move around like an ape moves.
3. This activity is easily broken into parts. If your class is learning a specific letter or group of letters, you can choose to do only the actions for those letters. Then, just enjoy reading the rest of the book to the children.
4. Following is a list of more great children's books with the alphabet as the theme:
    Chicka Chicka Boom Boom by Bill Martin Jr., and John Archambault
    Dr. Seuss's ABC: An Amazing Alphabet Book by Dr. Seuss
    Rainbow Fish A, B, C by Marcus Pfister

Syllable Freeze Dance

There are no outs or winners in this Freeze Dance! Teach the children to hear and know the sounds of one- and two-syllable words.

How to Do It

1. Tell the children that words have parts, called *syllables*. Examples of words with one part are *dog, cat, book, boy, run, skip,* or *fun*. Ask the children to give you more examples of words with one syllable.

2. Tell them that some words have two parts or syllables, such as *wiggle, pencil, notebook,* or *number*. Clap as you say the words, clapping on each syllable. Ask the children to give you some more examples of words with two syllables.

3. Invite the children to stand up and spread out in the open space of the room.

4. Tell them that when they hear a word with one syllable, such as *dog, cat, boy*, or *book*, that is the signal to dance.

5. Tell them that when they hear a word with two syllables, such as *pencil, buggy, notebook,* or *swingset,* that is the signal to freeze.

6. Call out a one-syllable word. Let them dance around for a few seconds, and then call out a two-syllable word and remind them to freeze.

7. Repeat several times so they get the idea, and then continue as long as the children are enjoying the game.

Expand It!

Allow volunteers to be the leader and call out one- and two-syllable words.

Singing and Clapping Rhythms

Clapping rhythms is a precursor to understanding syllables.

How to Do It

1. Choose a song with a simple rhythm to sing with the children, such as "Twinkle, Twinkle, Little Star."

2. Encourage them to clap or tap along with the rhythm as you sing:

    Twinkle, twinkle, little star,
    How I wonder what you are.
    Up above the world so high,
    Like a diamond in the sky,
    Twinkle, twinkle, little star,
    How I wonder what you are.

3. Sing the song again and have the children stand up and move their bodies and heads side to side as they clap and sing the words.

Act Out the Rhythm

Support children's understanding of syllables.

How to Do It

1. Ask the children to stand in a circle.

2. Tell children that when you call out a word, they should do the action of the word as many times as there are beats or syllables in that word.

3. Call out a verb, such as *hop*. Clap once as you say the word, and hold up one finger. Tell the children that this word has one beat, one syllable. Encourage them to hop one time.

4. Call out several more verbs with one syllable; for example, *spin, bounce, eat, stomp,* or *jump,* clapping once for the syllable. Then encourage the children to do that action one time.

5. Next, call out a verb with two syllables, such as *wiggle*. Clap two times for the two syllables. Hold up two fingers and encourage the children to do that action two times.

6. Call out several more words with two syllables; for example, *giggle, yawning, running, laughing, jumping, stomping,* or *bouncing.*

Tapping Our Names

Use the names of the children in your class to help them learn to identify syllables.

How to Do It

1. Ask the children to sit in a circle.
2. Start with one child and say her name out loud. As you say the syllables, tap on your knees. For example, say, "Sa-rah, Sa-rah, Sa-rah. Sarah has two syllables." Encourage the children to say that child's name and tap out the syllables in her name.
3. Move to the next child in the circle and say his name, tapping the syllables on your knees. For example, say, "Ben-ja-min, Ben-ja-min. How many syllables does Benjamin have? Yes, three. Let's tap out the syllables in Benjamin's name."
4. Continue around the circle, saying and tapping out the syllables in each child's name.

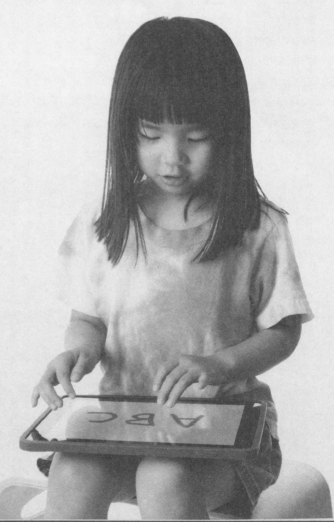

Rhythm around the Room

Choose objects around the room and clap out the syllables in the names.

How to Do It

1. Choose two one-syllable objects, such as chair and block, and two two-syllable objects, such as table and carpet, in your classroom.
2. Ask the children to listen for the number of sounds or syllables in the names of the objects. Say the names of each and clap out the syllables:
   Chair Clap once for one syllable
   Table Clap twice for two syllables
   Block Clap once for one syllable
   Carpet Clap twice for two syllables
3. Put together a pattern of syllables with the words: *chair, table, block, carpet*, one, one-two, one, one-two. Clap this rhythm with the children as you say the word pattern: *One, one-two, one, one-two, chair, ta-ble, block, car-pet.*
4. Stand up with the children and march around, clapping and stomping to the beat as you repeat the rhythm.
5. Choose four more objects and repeat the process, clapping and stomping to the beat as you repeat the word and syllable pattern.

Expand It!

Put the two patterns together to create a longer pattern. March around the room to this new rhythm pattern.

Animal Rhythms

Learn how many syllables are in animal names.

How to Do It

1. Ask the children to sit cross-legged in a circle.
2. Using the names of animals that your class has been studying or any animal names you wish, tap out the syllables of each animal's name on your knees: *snake, ti-ger, li-on, os-trich, mon-key, wil-de-beest, but-ter-fly, o-rang-u-tan, rhi-noc-er-os.*
3. Call out the list a second time, and have a volunteer stand up and act out each animal while the class taps out the rhythm of the animal's name.

Rhythms of Animal Sounds

Once the children have learned how to tap out the syllables of the animal names, tap out the sounds the animals make.

How to Do It

1. Invite the children to sit in a circle. Ask the children to name an animal and to tell you the sound that animal makes; for example, a kitten says, "Me-ow." Tap out on your knees the syllables in the sound that animal makes.

2. Ask the children to name other animals and tap out the syllables in the sounds those animals make. Alternatively, you can name the animals, and the children can tell you the sounds the animals make.

Tiger	*Roar*
Monkey	*Ee-Ee*
Kitten	*Me-ow*
Duck	*Quack*
Donkey	*Hee-haw*
Dog	*Woof*
Chicken	*Cluck*
Bird	*Chirp*
Frog	*Rib-bet*
Rooster	*Cock-a-doo-dle-doo*

3. For fun, repeat the exercise, using flopping fish feet to keep the rhythm of the syllables. Extend your legs out in front of you, and allow your feet to flop in and out like fish flopping on land.

Expand It!

Go around the circle and ask for volunteers to demonstrate tapping out the syllables and acting out the animals as they make the sounds. Ask the children how many syllables each sound has.

"Ing" Action Words

Words that end in –ing are happening! Children will enjoy this fun twist on Charades.

How to Do It

1. Ask the children to stand and spread out to give themselves plenty of room to move.
2. Explain that you will whisper an –ing word into each child's ear and then that child will act out the word.
3. Encourage the rest of the class to guess what word he is acting out. When someone guesses correctly, ask the whole class to act out the word.

Acting	Driving	Playing	Swimming
Biking	Eating	Rowing	Washing
Cleaning	Hugging	Running	Writing
Cooking	Jumping	Searching	
Dancing	Laughing	Singing	

4. Continue until each child has had a chance to act out an –ing word.

Green Goats Go

Help children connect letters with sounds.

How to Do It

1. Before the activity, create sets of words in these three categories: color, animal, and action. Each word in the set should have the same onset, for example:
   - Green Goats (or Geckos) Go
   - Blue Bats (or Baboons or Beavers) Bounce
   - Red Roosters (Rabbits, Rhinos) Run
   - Pink Pigs (Pandas, Porcupines) Play
   - White Whales (Walruses) Wiggle
   - Black Bears (Birds, Badgers) Bend

2. Ask the children to spread out a few feet apart so they will have room to move.

3. Give the children a color and an animal. Point out to them that the two words start with the same letter and the same sound. For example, say, "Blue bats. *Blue* and *bats* each start with the letter *B*. *B* makes the /b/ sound. Say it with me: /b/ /b/ blue, /b/ /b/ bats."

4. Next add an action. For example, say, "*Blue* and *bats* start with *B*. Blue bats bounce! *Bounce* starts with the letter *B*! /b/ /b/ Bounce!"

5. Encourage the children to act out how the animal moves: "Blue bats bounce! /b/ /b/ Blue /b/ /b/ bats /b/ /b/ bounce!"

6. Continue with your sets, and then let the children offer their suggestions once they get the hang of it.

I, He, She, We

Support learning and the use of personal pronouns.

How to Do It

1. Invite the children to sit in a circle. Begin with the personal pronoun *I*. Say a simple sentence such as, "I am washing my hands," and pretend to wash your hands. Ask the children who is washing her hands. They should eagerly tell you that you are the one who is washing her hands. Tell them that *I* means "me;" the person who is talking is also the one who is doing the action.

2. Offer a few more examples, saying the sentence and then acting it out:

    I am walking into school. (Pretend to be walking into school.)

    I am drinking some water. (Pretend to drink some water.)

    I am looking at a book. (Pretend to find a book and look at it.)

    Each time, ask the children who is doing the action.

3. Next, move on to *he* and *she*. Ask for a volunteer, and say a simple sentence such as, "He (or she) is looking at a book." Ask the volunteer to act out that sentence. Ask the children to tell you who is looking at a book. When they tell you, emphasize the pronoun and confirm that, yes, *he* (or *she*) is looking at a book.

4. Discuss that *he* means "a boy" and *she* means "a girl." Have boy volunteers take turns and stand up to act out some sentences. Then, ask girl volunteers to take turns acting out some sentences, such as the following:

    (He or she) is jumping in puddles. (Jump in puddles)

    (He or she) is finding shells on the beach. (Look for shells on the beach)

    (He or she) is twirling around. (Twirl around)

    (He or she) is dancing. (Dance around)

    (He or she) is sleeping. (Pretend to sleep)

Expand It!

If the children seem to have a firm understanding of *I, he,* and *she,* try expanding to the plural *we*. Discuss that *we* means a group, such as the class, that includes the person who is talking.

Have children stand in a circle and act out the following sentences:

    We are holding hands in a circle. (Hold hands in a circle)

    We are going round and round in a circle. (Go round and round)

    We are jumping all together in a circle. (Jump, holding hands)

    We are going into the circle to make it small (Hold hands in a circle and all move in to make the circle smaller)

    We are moving out wide to make the circle big. (Move wide to make the circle larger again)

A Sentence Tells a Little Story

This activity supports the understanding of basic sentence structure.

How to Do It

1. Tell the children that a sentence is a group of words that go together to give a complete idea. Explain that by themselves the words cannot do much, but all together they make sense and tell a little story.

2. Ask the children to stand. Choose a word to be your subject, such as *cat*. Tell the children that, when you say *cat,* they are to freeze in a cat pose. Look at the children and say, "Cat."

3. Pick an action word that goes with the subject. Tell the class that you will give them an action to do as cats. Say, for example, *jumps, skips, wiggles, hops,* or *crawls,* and let the children act out that verb.

4. Ask them to freeze in a cat pose again. Tell them you will give them a descriptive word to tell how the cat is moving—an adverb. Offer an adverb, such as *fast, slowly, crazily,* or *sleepily.*

5. Say the whole sentence, pausing between words. Encourage the children to act out the sentence: *The cat* (pause) *crawls* (pause) *slowly* (pause).

6. Put the three parts together without pauses and let the children act out the sentence. Pause at the end of the sentence, and say, "That is a sentence!"

7. Change the adverbs to let the children act out the sentences in different ways. Ask the class, "How did the cat crawl?" Let them answer you.

Expand It!

Encourage the children to take turns making their own sentences. Give them a subject, and ask them to offer sentences for the class to act out.

Open Your Book

This activity uses fine and gross motor skills, cross-body patterning, quantitative thinking, and addition to help children connect to reading a book.

How to Do It

1. This simple exercise can be done standing or sitting, in a line, a circle, or in the children's own spaces around the room.

2. Ask the children to watch you as you show them what to do:

    One hand and one hand (Put up one hand, palm out, and then the other hand)

    Clap (Clap hands together once)

    One hand and one hand (Put up one hand, then the other hand)

    Make two hands (Clap hands together once)

    Open your book! (Open palms of hands like a book)

    Let's see what's in our book today!

3. Add to the action by using the arms and legs. Get the whole body involved!

    Ready? (Stand straight and tall with feet together, arms and hands by your sides.)

    Open your book! (Stand with legs wide apart and arms and hands out to sides in a T shape)

    Turn the page! (Cross left hand over with a big arm movement, and touch the palm of the right hand)

    Hold the page—one! (Use the fingers of the left hand to mime lifting a page

    And open—two! Mime turning a page by making an arc back over to the other side. Children's hands will be back in the T shape of open arms and hands and feet.)

    Let's see what's in our book today!

4. You can do the action while seated, as well:

    Ready? (Sit on the floor with knees up and together. Hands on knees.)

    Open your book! (Open the position of the knees outward toward the floor. Place the hands on top of the thighs with palms facing up.)

    Turn the page! (Cross the left hand over and touch the palm of the right hand.)

    Hold the page—one! (Use the fingers of the left hand to mime lifting and turning a page.)

    And open—two! (Making a big arc back over to the other side. Children's hands will be back in the starting position.)

    Let's see what's in our book today!

The Beginning, the Middle, and the End

Children love to act out stories. Talk about the meaning of the words *beginning, middle,* and *end*: The *beginning* is the start where you find out what could happen; the *middle* is what happens to make the story; the *end* is the last thing the story tells you.

How to Do It

1. Read any children's book to the class. This activity works well with any story.
2. Ask the children to sit or stand in the middle of the room. Choose an action from the beginning of the story. Teach that action to the class, and show them where it is in the book. Have children do the action. For example, in *Goodnight Moon* by Margaret Wise Brown, the bunny rabbit gets in bed and looks at his telephone and a red balloon. Ask the children to pretend to get into bed and look around for a telephone and a red balloon.
3. Pick an important action from the middle of the story that advances the plot significantly. Identify the action to the class and show them where it is in the book. Again, have children do the action. In *Goodnight Moon,* the bunny rabbit says goodnight to things in his room, pointing at the objects: the pictures on the wall, the comb and brush, the moon, and the cow. Ask the children to pretend to do these actions.
4. Pick an action that closes the story and brings it to an end. Identify the action to the class, and show them where it is in the book. Have children do the action. In *Goodnight Moon*, the bunny rabbit goes to sleep. Ask the children to pretend to go to sleep.
5. Put the actions all together in consecutive order, reinforcing the story order.

Expand It!

Have children take turns showing their own choices of three actions for the beginning, the middle, and the end.

Follow Me

This activity reinforces the concept of sequencing, as it follows a single character through a story. By stringing the actions together, children see how the character makes the story happen in a logical sequence, an action version of the way in which turning the pages of the book advances the story from beginning to end.

How to Do It

1. Choose a story to read to the class, such as *Are You My Mother?* by P. D. Eastman.
2. Ask the children to spread out and stand in the middle of the room.
3. Pick three actions that the character does throughout the story (in order of occurrence). In our example:
   - The baby bird pops out of the egg in his nest. (Children pretend to pop out of an egg.)
   - The baby bird walks around looking for his mother, asking birds, animals, and machines if they are his mother. (Children walk around, pretending to look for their mother.)
   - The baby bird gets dropped back in his nest where his mother finds him. (Children pretend to be dropped back into the nest.)
4. Direct the class through each of the three actions, pausing in between to have time for creativity and movement invention. If needed, give the children verbal cues to act out each action, and then put the actions in order one after the other without pausing, moving to act out a series of actions that happen to that character throughout the story.

Expand It!

1. Read the story again; only this time, tell the children that you will add an action for the children to perform as you retell the story.
2. Choose the initial three actions and then discuss with the class and have children pick another action the main character does within the story.
3. As the children become comfortable with this activity, lengthen the number of actions chosen or choose larger and smaller movements for contrast.

What Do We Do Together?

This activity also reinforces the quantitative math concept of a pair and the one-to-one math concept of two. It works with any story that has just two characters. Help the children notice how two characters interact with each other to make a story—what happens in a book when two characters do things together?

How to Do It

1. Choose a book to read to the children, such as *Moonbear's Dream* by Frank Asch. Read the story to the seated group, pointing out each of the two characters—in this case, Bear and Little Bird.

2. Ask children how they think the characters are relating to each other or making actions happen. Listen as they share their ideas.

3. Pick four actions from each of the two main characters within a story, in the order of occurrence. For example:

    Little Bird shows Bear he sees a kangaroo jumping through the yard.

    Bear sees the kangaroo, too, and decides they must be dreaming.

    Bear scoops honey from his honey jar.

    Little Bird eats birdseed.

    Bear drops the honey jar and makes a mess.

    Little Bird pushes the flower vase off the table and makes a mess.

    Bear and Little Bird are surprised to come back to the house to find it neat and clean.

    Bear goes to sleep in his bed, and Little Bird goes to sleep in his drawer.

    For a shorter exercise, pick only two actions for each character.

4. Children then stand in the middle of the room as a group (spread arm's-length apart to have space) to move through the actions.

5. Ask the children to move to represent the actions of the characters. They may do this in a number of ways:

    - Children go back and forth between the two characters, acting each of them out in turn.
    - Children take turns being one character or another.
    - Place children into two groups, and each group represents a specific character.

6. Direct the class through each action for each character in the order they occur in the story, pausing between each action. Give the class verbal cues for each action, as needed.
7. Put the actions in order, one after another, without pausing.

Expand It!

1. If appropriate for your group, choose more than four actions per character.
2. Fully act out the story by reading it and doing movements.

What Do We Do as a Group?

The activity reinforces the quantitative math concepts of group (many) and one.

How to Do It

1. Choose a story to read to the children. The activity works with any story that has several characters; but to emphasize the concept of a group, it is helpful to choose a story in which there is one character separate from the group. For our example, we will use *The Perfect Little Monster* by Judy Hinsley.

2. Help the children recognize the group, in this case, the monster family. Help them recognize the individual, in this case, the baby monster.

3. Ask the children to spread out in the middle of the room. Ask for a volunteer to be the baby monster, or the teacher or classroom aide can be the baby.

4. Read or tell the story again, asking the children to move in response to each action.
   - The baby monster sits on his blanket and scowls, howls, and makes a mess.
   - The monster family loves him and teaches him how to snarl and make a bigger mess.
   - The monster family has a big first birthday party for the baby monster.
   - The baby monster smiles during his party, and his family shrieks because they like scowls better than smiles.

5. The children can take turns being the Other Character who interacts with the group to move the story forward.

Expand It!

Add other characters in a story that interact with the group and move the story forward.

The Five Ws: Who? What? Where? When? Why?

This activity helps children learn the five important questions to answer when reading any book.

How to Do It

1. Choose a story to read to the children as they sit in a circle. For our example, we will use *The Foolish Tortoise* by Richard Buckley.

2. As you read, ask the children to listen for the answers to five questions about the story: who, what, where, when, and why. **Who** is the main character? **What** does that character do? **Where** does the character live? **When** does the story take place? **Why** does the character do the actions?

3. Provide a selection of props for the children to use as they act out the answers to the five questions.

4. When you finish reading, tell the children they will now be the character, or characters, in the book, and act out the answers to the five questions.

5. Ask children to answer the five *W* questions. After each answer, children can stand up and take a trip around you in a circle, doing the actions.

   ● Who? The Tortoise, green with a shell on his back.
   The class becomes Tortoise, miming having a shell and moving around the circle the way the Tortoise moves.

   ● What? The Tortoise takes off his shell and has adventures until he puts the shell back on.
   The class does an action to represent one of the Tortoise's adventures.

   ● Where? The Tortoise is walking on land, near a river, under sun, in rain and wind, and under a moon.
   The class pretends to move in these environments. How would a tortoise move on land? Near a river? in the sun? in the rain? in the wind? under a moon?

   ● When? The Tortoise starts the adventures in the day and ends at night.
   The class moves like a tortoise in daytime and at night.

   ● Why? The Tortoise is tired of his shell and wants to have adventures.
   The class moves to represent the Tortoise taking off his shell.

6. Then put all of these actions together. Call out the questions, answers, and actions as you go along. As you prompt them with questions, ask the children to do the actions of the story. You can continue to have children move around you in the circle, or take the children on a trip through the classroom and create a larger environment for the action of the story.

Actions Make the Story

This activity reinforces listening skills and motor skills, as the children learn that many actions move a story forward from beginning to end.

How to Do It

1. Choose a book to read in which a sequence of actions is important, such as *Mike Mulligan and His Steam Shovel* by Virginia Lee Burton.
2. First, read the book to the class, asking the children to listen for the actions that happen in the story.
3. Teach the actions. You can use as few or as many actions as you choose, depending on the amount of time you would like for an exercise. This is a teacher-only script where you will identify the actions and then tell the class what they will do to make the action sequences:
   - Pretend to be steam shovels, digging up the ground.
   - Drive the steam shovel on roads.
   - Drive the steam sholvel up and down, over the hills.
   - Dig around the room, marking out corners for a square shape.
4. Read the story again slowly. Have children do each action sequence after reading each page that shows the action.

Expand It!

Read a book and take suggestions from the class to do three actions.

What Happens Next?

This activity helps children see how cause and effect go together to make a story—the beginning of logical thinking. Convey the excitement of reading by keeping children guessing and acting out what happens next!

How to Do It

1. Choose a book to read to the children, such as *Curious George* by H. A. and Margaret Rey.

2. Read the beginning of the story. Stop at the place in which you can introduce a problem or situation that the main character must solve or act upon.

3. Have children stand up and do the main character's action. For example, in *Curious George,* George finds and puts on a yellow hat. Ask the children to show how he might put on the hat.

4. Ask the children, *What do you think will happen next? What will happen because the character took this action?* Encourage the children to make suggestions, and discuss their suggestions with them.

5. Have children try out their ideas all at once. Then lead the group in trying several of the action ideas all together. After the children have had a chance to try out their ideas, ask them to stop and sit down.

6. Next, ask the children to sit and listen as you read the middle part of the story. Say, *This is what we know the character did. Let's see what happens next.* Continue reading to show the children what happens. Help the children make the connection between the character's action and the effect. In *Curious George,* George puts on the hat, and then he gets captured.

7. Stop after reading the effect. Ask the children to act out the cause (George puts on the yellow hat.) and the effect (George gets captured.)

8. After the children have had a chance to do the cause-and-effect actions, ask them to sit down. Continue reading, connecting causes (actions on the part of the main character) with effects. Let the children act out the causes and effects.

More Book Ideas

The Snowy Day by Ezra Jack Keats

If You Give a Mouse a Cookie by Laura Numeroff

This Happens Because

Learning how cause and effect, or "the because," works in stories and helps build the beginnings of logical thought patterns.

How to Do It

1. Select a story to read to the children, such as *The Mitten* by Jan Brett, which includes a clear cause and effect.

2. Pause after you have read the action that is a cause. For example, in *The Mitten*, one of Nikki's mittens falls off when he climbs a tree while playing in the snow. Ask the children to notice what happens.

3. Ask the children to get up as a group and use actions to show what the character is doing. In our example, the children become Nikki, doing the actions of putting on his mitten, going outside to play, and having the mitten fall off his hand as he climbs a tree. Reaffirm their actions: *So that's what Nikki is doing. One of his mittens falls off while he climbs a tree.*

4. After the children have had a chance to mimic the character's actions, ask them to sit back down to listen.

5. Continue reading the story, reading the effect that the character's action has. Discuss briefly with the children what happens *because* of the character's action.

6. Ask the children to get up as a group and use actions to show what happens. In our example, the children become the mitten, falling into the snow, and getting stretched bigger and bigger as more and more animals crawl inside it. Reaffirm the children's actions: *Because Nikki loses his mitten while he climbs a tree, the mitten falls in the snow and gets stretched bigger and bigger as more and more animals crawled inside it to get warm and cozy.*

7. Next, put the two actions together: *Because the character does this, this is what happens in the story.* Ask the children to use the movements to explore how the cause had an effect on the characters in the story.

8. When they have had a chance to perform their actions, ask them to sit back down and listen as you finish the story.

9. At the end of the story, reinforce the lesson: *So, because one of Nikki's mittens falls off while he climbed a tree, what happens?* Have the children tell you what happens while they show you with the action. *Right. Because Nikki loses his mitten while he climbs a tree, the mitten falls in the snow and gets stretched bigger and bigger as more and more animals crawl inside it to get warm and cozy.*

Expand It!

Choose up to three cause-and-effect sequences from a book to extend the exercise.

Repeat It!

This activity helps the children develop listening skills as they learn how a key word, phrase, or sentence makes the point of the story and moves the story forward.

How to Do It

1. Choose a story that features a repeated word, phrase, or sentence, such as *Guess How Much I Love You* by Sam McBratney.

2. Before reading the story to the children, tell them the word, phrase, or sentence to listen for, and teach them a simple action to stand and do when they hear that word, phrase, or sentence. In our example, when Big Nutbrown Hare tells Little Nutbrown Hare he loves him, ask the children to try to stretch all the way to the moon and back. When they have finished saying the word, phrase, or sentence while doing the action, have the class sit back down and you can continue reading the book.

3. As you read the book, help the children recognize the word, phrase, or sentence the first time it occurs. Ask the children: *And what do you think happens next?* This is the cue for the class to stand up and do the action while saying the word, phrase, or sentence with you.

4. Continue reading, cuing the class if needed. After a few times, the children may be able to do the action and say the word, phrase, or sentence by themselves.

Expand It!

You can add some of the actions that follow from the word, phrase, or sentence. For example, in *Guess How Much I Love You,* after Big Nutbrown Hare tells Little Nutbrown Hare he loves him, they hop around together. The children can add the hopping action before sitting down again until the next time the phrase occurs.

The Magic World of Silence

This activity reinforces listening skills, watching skills, and motor skills, including fine-motor hand and finger motions. The calm that the silence represents can also extend to children, providing a feeling of calm watchfulness and attention.

How to Do It

1. Choose a book to read that includes detailed actions, such as *Scupper the Sailor Dog* by Margaret Wise Brown.

2. Introduce the children to the concept of *miming*: making movements without words. The idea of mime is to slow down the action to see how you do it. To help them understand, practice a few simple movements, such as the following:
   - writing or drawing
   - opening and closing a window
   - brushing teeth
   - opening and shutting a door
   - peeling a banana or orange
   - climbing a tree

3. Ask the children to sit in a line or circle. Introduce the class to the Magic World of Silence where, instead of talking, everyone is quiet and showing the actions of the story instead of talking: *Now we are going to go into the Magic World of Silence! Shhh!* Ask the children to take three deep breaths in and out and to listen to the quiet in the room. Your room does not need to be silent, but the idea of silence creates a unique atmosphere!

4. Read the book so the class can recognize specific actions a character does with objects in settings. As you read, talk about what actions the character uses and what the setting is for the actions. In *Scupper the Sailor Dog*, for example, Scupper uses his fingers to carefully hang his hat, rope, and pants on one hook in the cabin of his little boat. He hangs his coat and spyglass on other hooks.

5. After reading the story, pick three actions from the book the class can mime in detail. Do the three actions together as a class. For example, Scupper puts his shoes away and gets into a bunk bed. He moves his saw back and forth to cut wood and build a house. He finds a stick, makes it into a fishing pole with a string on it, and uses it to catch a fish in a river.

6. Read the story again, pausing at the appropriate moments to let the children mime the actions.

Extend It!

Each child can take a turn and pick one action to show the class. It can be any action from the book that the child remembers.

Let's Find the Character

This activity supports learning of prepositional phrases and works well with lift-the-flap books and other books that ask the reader to look for a character.

How to Do It

1. Select a lift-the-flap or find-the-character book to read to the children, such as *Where's Spot?* by Eric Hill.

2. Tell the children they will be looking for the character throughout the book. Begin reading, stopping at the flaps or on each page to look for the character.

3. As you look with the children, use prepositional phrases to indicate where the character may be hiding: *under the table, behind the door, in the closet, on a box,* and so on. Help the children, as necessary, to understand what these phrases mean.

4. Create actions to accompany the places where children look in the book; for example, if the children look under a table, ask them to do an "under the table" action.

5. Extend the actions to your classroom. As you read, ask the children to get up and look in the location you name. When the character is not there, say: *Not there! But what do we see there?*

6. Ask the children to return to their seats on the floor, and show them in the book what is in the place where they looked for the character.

7. Continue reading the book, using prepositional phrases and looking for the character, both in the book and in your classroom.

Expand It!

Make your own lift-the-flap pictures or books. For each child, paste a sheet of paper with a cut-out flap on top of another sheet, and have children draw who is hiding under the flap.

Figure It Out

Use this activity to help children develop problem-solving skills

How to Do It

1. Choose a book to read in which a character has a problem that needs to be solved, such as *If You Give a Mouse a Cookie* by Laura Numeroff.

2. Read the book to the children. As you reach each problem that the character must solve, stop and ask the children to offer ideas for how the character could solve the problem. For example, as the mouse eats the cookie, he becomes thirsty. What would the children do to help?

3. Try out the ideas using actions, all together as a group. Take three ideas to start. Have children take turns saying their solutions out loud and doing those actions with the whole group.

4. Ask the children to sit down again and listen as you continue reading the book to see how the main character solves the problem.

5. Compare the solution with the children's ideas you explored. Do the actions for the book solution, and then do the actions for the class ideas. How are they the same or different?

Stories Told Backward

This activity helps the children learn the logic of the progression in a story.

How to Do It

1. Choose a story to tell that has a logical progression of events, such as "Jack and Jill."
2. Choose three clear actions from the beginning, the middle, and the end of a story that the children will quickly understand. Tell children you will do a backward silly story.
3. Teach them the end action, the middle action, and then the beginning action. For example, in "Jack and Jill," the events in reverse order might be as follows:
   - Jack fell down and broke his crown, and Jill came tumbling after.
   - Fetch a pail of water.
   - Go up the hill.
   Do the actions in that order.
4. Ask the children if the story makes sense in that order. Encourage them to explain why it does or does not. You can repeat the actions again for fun.
5. Do the actions in the correct order, and then tell the correct version of the story to reinforce the idea of a logical progression.

Feelings Show the Story

This activity helps children learn how a character's feelings make a story and influence what happens in a story.

How to Do It

1. Choose a book to read in which a character expresses feelings, such as *Owl Babies* by Martin Waddell.
2. Read the book to the class. As you get to a part of the story where a character has a strong feeling, ask the children how that character is feeling and what that character might do because of that feeling. In our example, the owl babies come out of their nest onto the branches of the tree. They are sad and scared because their mother has left to find food.
3. Have the children stand up and do an action that illustrates the feelings the characters have. Let the children express the feelings that they are exploring. Use the setting of the book to suggest where the children imagine themselves to be and how they might move in those settings.
4. Ask the children to sit down while you continue to read. At appropriate points in the book, stop and ask them how the character might be feeling.
5. Ask the children to stand up and act out how they think the character is feeling and what the character will do because of those feelings. For example, in *Owl Babies*, the owl babies comfort each other by sitting close on the same branch and are so happy when their mother returns.

Expand It!

1. Ask the children to take turns showing their actions to the class.
2. Read a book such as *It's Okay to Be Different* by Todd Parr, and play some music that matches the mood of the book. Encourage the children to move to the music.

How Do You Feel?

Preschoolers understand and show feelings through actions more easily than through words. Encourage children to recognize the choices a character makes and to see the consequences of those choices. Then, give them an opportunity to explore the feelings through action. The children will be able to experience those feelings in a subtle and contained way, and you will have a chance to discuss those feelings and situations with the class.

How to Do It

1. Choose a book to read to the children, such as *Where the Wild Things Are* by Maurice Sendak or *Lilly's Purple Plastic Purse* by Kevin Henkes.
2. As you read, talk about what actions the character uses. For example, what does Max choose to do? How does his mother react to his choice?
3. Talk about the feelings of the characters in relation to the other characters. Ask the children to talk about how they think Max feels when he is sent to his room. Is he angry or sad or frustrated?
4. Ask the children to stand and show with their actions how the character is feeling. For example, encourage them to show how Max might be feeling when he is sent to his room. Remind them that, instead of talking, they should show with their bodies how they think Max feels.
5. When the children have had a chance to explore the emotion with their actions, ask them to sit down to listen to more of the story.
6. Continue reading, stopping to ask the children to act out how the character is feeling as the story progresses. It is not necessary to read the entire book in one sitting. Depending on the needs of the children in your class, you may wish to break the story into parts and read it over several days.

Expand It!

Have children take turns showing their action responses to the character's emotion.

What's the Problem?

In this activity, children learn about and "solve" the problem or obstacle that the characters in a story face.

How to Do It

1. This activity works well with any folktale or fairy tale, such as *The Three Billy Goats Gruff.*

2. Read or simply tell the story to the children.

3. Ask the children to identify the problem that the characters have. In our example, the goats want to cross the bridge, but the troll will not let them.

4. Teach the children one to three key lines, and have them do the actions that occur before and after the lines. Children do this exercise all together so that they are all doing the same character at the same time. For example, in *The Three Billy Goats Gruff*, the children pretend to be the goats, and they say, "Wait for my brother. He is bigger."

5. Tell the story to the children again. When you get to the part where the first goat meets the troll, ask the children to act out what he is doing:

    Pretend to be the youngest goat crossing over the bridge. He is stopped by the troll. The littlest goat says, "Wait for my brother. He is bigger." And he gets across and gallops away.

6. Continue to the second goat.

    Be the second, bigger goat crossing over the bridge. He is stopped by the troll. The second goat says, "Wait for my brother. He is bigger." And he gets across and gallops away.

7. Finally, tell the last part:

    Be the third and biggest goat crossing over the bridge. He is stopped by the troll. The big goat gallops with his head butting toward the troll. The troll runs away. The big goat walks across the bridge, and the three goats eat grass on the hillside.

Act It Out!

Read or tell a whole fairy tale or folktale, letting the children act out the parts using key lines and actions. Every child will get to participate in this fun way to tell a story.

How to Do It

1. Choose a folktale or fairytale to read or tell the children, such as *The Three Billy Goats Gruff*.

2. Choose key characters and lines of the tale; limit the number of characters to four and the number of lines to ten. For our example, you would need the children to pretend to be the three goats and a troll.

3. Tell the story, asking the children to act out the story as you tell it. Help the children by giving them their lines. Let the children decide how to do the actions. Go slowly, giving the children time to say their lines and show the actions.

4. Have children take turns being the characters. When a child has said the line and completed the action, he returns to the circle and another child then gets a turn.

5. The children who are waiting for a turn sit in the circle and repeat a narration line you give them to say, as a chorus. The chorus can tap out the rhythm with their hands on their knees as they say their line. For example, the chorus may say, "'Trip, trap, trip, trap!' went the bridge," as each goat crosses to the other side.

Expand It!

After you have done the tale a few times, children can also participate by being objects in the story. In *The Three Billy Goats Gruff*, for example, the group of children can stand up and connect their arms to be the bridge.

A Tale of Mixed-Up Letters

This fun and silly activity helps children become aware of how words sound and how letters form to make the sounds and meaning of words.

How to Do It

1. Choose a familiar story or tale to read or tell the children, such as *The Three Bears*.
2. Tell the children you will tell a funny, mixed-up version of the story, where the first letters and parts of some words will move around to different places.
3. When you get to a place in the story where the letters or mixed-up word sounds have jumped around, say, "Time to move!" Children get up and change their places in the room, acting like the characters as they move.
4. You can explain the mixed-up letters and words to them. After a few times, they will know it!

The Three Bears, **All Mixed Up**

Once a time upon, there lived in the woods three bears. There was the boppa pear, the bomma mear, and the little bearby babe.

Time to move! Move like the bears, and change your seat!

Now, these bears lived happily for a long time. Things were fine until one morning when they sat down to eat. You see, the boppa pear said, "My porridge is hoo tot!"

And the bomma mear tasted her porridge and said, "My porridge is hoo tot!"

And the little bearby babe said, "My porridge is hoo tot, too!"

So the bears decided to go for a long woods in the walk, to let their porridge cool.

Time to move! Move like the bears, and change your seat.

Well, as soon as they had gone, there came a knock knock knock, at the door. And do you know who that was? Right! It was a girl named Goldilocks.

Goldilocks went into the house, and she found three bowls of porridge, so she tasted them. Now, the first was hoo tot, and the second was hoo tot.

Time to move! Move like Goldilocks and change your seat.

But, the third bowl of porridge was just right! And Goldilocks was very hungry, so she ate it up!

And then she wanted to take a nap. So, Goldilocks looked for a bed. Up some stairs, she saw there were three little beds.

Now, the first bed was hoo tard.

And the second bed was soo toft.

But the third little bed was just right, so she lay down and fell fast asleep.

Time to move! Move like Goldilocks, and find a place to lie down on the floor.

Well, just then, the three bears came home!

And the boppa pear said, "Someone's been eating my porridge!"

The bomma mear said, "Someone's been eating my porridge!"

And the little bearby babe said, "Hey, someone's been eating my porridge, and there is monore, monore, monore for me! Waaa!"

Time to move! Move like the baby bear! He's crying! Find a seat.

Then, the three bears went upstairs.

And the boppa pear said, "Someone's been sleeping in my bed!"

The bomma mear said, "Someone's been sleeping in my bed!"

The little bearby babe said, "Someone's been sleeping in my bed, and there she is!"

So Goldilocks jumped up and ran all the way home!

Time to move! Move like Goldilocks! Run home and find a seat in our circle!

But at least she had had a good breakfast. Those bears made good cereal!

The End

Look At Me, I Can Be . . .

Encourage positive self-image and confidence through the creation and ownership of a character.

How to Do It

1. Teach the class the following poem:
    Turn around
    Count to three
    Look at me
    I Can Be a _____.
    And this is how I do it.

2. Ask for a volunteer. Ask the child to think of a character, such as a firefighter or dancer, and help her as she says the poem and does the actions:
    Turn around (Turn around and around)
    Count to three (Class counts, "One, two, three!" with the child)
    Look at me (Child stops turning and faces the class)
    I Can Be a _____. (Child says what she is)
    And this is how I do it. (Child moves as the character to show who the character is)

3. Encourage the class to stand up and try it with the child: "Look, we all do it our own way. Everybody can do this. Every person's body does it in its own way."
    The children stand up and become the kind of character their classmate has shown, moving in their own ways.

4. Continue until each child has had a turn. Some examples of who the children can be include the following: ballerina, fireman, crossing guard, bulldozer driver, hip-hop dancer, doctor, prince, princess, football player, computer person, store clerk, plumber, or any character the children can dream up!

Extend It!

Read *Whoever You Are* by Mem Fox to the children.

A Child's Own 20-Second Story: "My Morning"

We all have stories to tell. This activity helps children own the idea that their stories have meaning and importance, too, just as those in books do. This connects children to the idea of books as natural parts of their day and not something "other." Even their daily routines make a story.

How to Do It

1. Be sensitive to the individual stories in your class, and take care to do this exercise in a way in which each child can feel good about her story. Know your children's morning histories before you do this exercise. If a few children have a very different morning routine from the others, emphasize something positive about that routine. It is important to maintain the anti-bullying tone of the exercise.

2. Tell the children they will make their own stories about the three things they did before getting to school. Adjust the activity to your class's actual morning routines: what kinds of clothes they put on, where (when and how or if) they have breakfast, how they get to school, and what they see on their way to school.

3. First, do the story as a group, and tell children three details you have chosen. For example, you could start out with this sample story:

    This morning, we all got up and got ready to go to school! What did we do to get ready?

    > First, we woke up and got ready for school. (Act out waking, rising, dressing, and so on.) Then, we ate breakfast. (Pretend to eat.) Next we went to school. (Wave hello to our friends and our teacher.)

4. Let each child take a turn telling his story. Encourage each child to act out parts of his story, and prompt the child with a few questions to help him remember details. (Some children will be able to say and act out the story pattern themselves.)

Expand It!

Read *Corduroy's Day* by Don Freeman to the children. This book identifies the routine by action and by number.

Creating a Character

Use this activity to help children create an original character for their own stories, using imagination and details, and letting the character tell the story through actions.

How to Do It

1. Tell children they will make their own characters, just like a character in a book, to tell their own stories. As their character, they can become anyone or anything they wish. They can have superpowers; they can move, look, or sound like an animal or a machine. They can be anything or anyone!

2. Ask the children to close their eyes and think of who or what they want to be! Ask them questions that will help them think about their characters:
   - Who is your character?
   - What does your character look like?
   - How does your character move?
   - How does your character sound?

   Encourage children to use their imaginations.

3. When the children have a character in mind, ask them to stand up like their characters would stand. Ask them to take a pose just like their characters would.

4. Ask them to walk just like their character walks. Do they take giant steps or tiny steps? Do they move on their hands and knees or on tiptoe? Do they hop?

5. Let the children walk around in character for a few minutes, and then ask them to freeze. Ask: "How high can your character jump?" Let them show you, and then ask them to freeze.

6. Ask: "Does your character have any special powers?" Let the children demonstrate their characters' special powers.

7. Ask: "How big can your character smile? Or, is your character mad or sad?" Give the children time to react as their characters would. Ask: "Does your character laugh? If so, does your character laugh loudly or softly?" Give the children time to laugh (or not) in character.

8. Encourage the children to move around as their characters and to show all of the things their characters can do. Remind them to please use their seeing eyes and listening ears.

9. After creating their characters, let the children take turns to say who their character is. Or, have small groups become characters while the rest of the class watches. Do this by inviting three to five children at a time to go into the center of the room and create a character. This is a good way to build acceptance and to understand and be empowered by individuality.

Expand It!

- Read a one-character book that is highly descriptive, such as *Gingerbread Man Superhero!* By Dotti Enderle or *Ladybug Girl* by David Soman and Jacky Davis, and ask the class to point out the characteristics of the main character.

Show and Tell

Children use everyday objects they find in the classroom—toys, trucks, musical instruments, pencils, books, and so on—to create a story with movement.

How to Do It

1. Tell children they will show (by moving) and tell (by speaking) a story about a small object they have with them or can find in the classroom. Help the children find an object such as a favorite toy, a tool such as a sand shovel, or any other object they wish to use.

2. Demonstrate, using an item such as a pencil:

    This is my pencil.

    I can find it on my desk in a special cup.

    I like it because I can write words that I want to say.

    And I can show you what it does! (Pantomime writing with the pencil.)

    Let's all get up and do what my pencil can do! (Children stand up and do the action that the pencil is doing.)

3. Encourage the children to take turns standing up and telling a story about their objects, complete with movements to show what the object can do.

Expand It!

Read a book to the children about a special item, such as *The Keeping Quilt* by Patricia Palacco (a story about a quilt that reminds its owners of home), or a book about show and tell, such as *Show and Tell Day* by Anne Rockwell.

A Child's Own Tall Tale

Children use their imaginations to make up a silly tall tale to share with the class. Through call and response, the children sharpen their listening and social-awareness skills.

How to Do It

1. Tell the children they will use their imaginations to make up a silly tall tale that they can act out together. Explain that a tall tale is a story that is so silly that everyone who reads or hears it knows it is pure imagination!

2. To help the children understand what to do, tell them that you will tell your own tall tale:

   Do you know? There is a hippo in my yard, and it is digging up potatoes there!
   Class: What? *A hippo!*
   Class: Where? *In my yard!*
   Class: What's it doing there? *It is digging for potatoes there! It likes to eat potatoes!*

3. Encourage the children to stand up and pretend to be hippos digging up and eating potatoes.

4. Offer some other examples, such as the following, or let the children make up their own tall tales:

   - *There is an elephant on my street, and it is reaching for peanuts.*
   - *There is a monkey in my bedroom, and it is picking bananas.*
   - *There is a snake in my yard, and it is digging up carrots.*
   - *There is a turtle in my bathtub, and it is diving for seaweed.*

5. Give each child a turn to make up a tall tale and act it out with the class.

The Class Creates a Story

Help the children understand story structure by creating a story as a group, making choices of what to put in and doing actions that show the story.

How to Do It

1. Tell children they will create a story all together. You can create several short stories by taking several suggestions, or you can create a longer story by taking suggestions from each child.

2. Ask the children to answer the Five *W* questions: *who, what, where, when*, and *why*. You can use these questions to keep children interested in what comes next.

3. Ask the children to sit in a circle. Ask a volunteer, "Who will we be in our story?" If, for example, the child suggests, "Dragons!" let that child lead the children on a trip around the circle being dragons.

4. Ask the next volunteer, "What are we doing?" In our example, the child responds, "Looking for a magic flower!" Let that child lead the others around the circle as dragons looking for magic flowers.

5. Continue, asking the questions and letting the children act out the suggestions as the story builds:

   "Where are we going to do it?" (Possible response: In a fern-filled forest; the children pretend to be dragons looking for magic flowers in a fern-filled forest.)

   "When are we doing it?" (Possible response: Early in the morning; the children pretend to be dragons stretching early in the morning.)

   "Why do we want to do it?" (Possible response: to bring the flower to a friend; the children pretend to be dragons bringing magic flowers to each other.)

Expand It!

For a longer exercise, each child can make his whole quick story. Have a child answer the five questions and lead the group on a trip around the circle to act out the story.

Bounce to the Rhythm of the Rhyme

Use movement to help children learn how to recognize rhythm in a rhyme.

How to Do It

1. Ask the children to stand in a big circle and place their hands on their hips.
2. Begin by reciting a rhyme and bounce your knees to the beat. You can use any nursery rhyme with this exercise. Bounce on the boldface words:

   Little Miss **Muffet**
   Sat on a **tuffet**,
   Eating her **curds** and **whey**.
   Along came a **spider**,
   Who **sat** down **beside** her
   And **frightened** Miss **Muffet** away.
3. Repeat the exercise, this time having everyone recite the rhyme aloud.

Move to the Rhythm of the Poem

Help the children feel the meter or rhythm of a poem as they move to the words.

How to Do It

1. This is different from just moving freely to music. The meter of a poem is felt in their bodies and associated with words and phrases. Choose any poem with a definite meter, and encourage the children to move freely to the rhythm, responding to it as they wish.

2. Set up a swaying motion and children will stay within the rhythm naturally. You keep the swaying motion going with your hand as the children stop swaying and move freely.

   Mary had a little lamb, (Sway four times)

   Little lamb, little lamb. (Sway four times)

   Mary had a little lamb (Sway four times)

   whose fleece was white as snow. (Sway four times)

3. Continue as long as the children are engaged in moving to the rhythm.

Clap to the Rhythm

Clapping is an easy way to help children identify the rhythm pattern of a poem or song.

How to Do It

1. Choose any poem or song that the children enjoy.
2. Clap to the rhythm:
   Mary had a little lamb (clap four times)
   Little lamb (clap two times)
   Little lamb (clap two times)
   Mary had a little lamb (clap four times)
   Her fleece was white as snow. (clap three times)
   Everywhere that Mary went (clap four times)
   Mary went (clap two times)
   Mary went (clap two times)
   Everywhere that Mary went (clap four times)
   Her lamb was sure to go. (clap three times)

Clap in the Rest

The pause between lines of a song or poem is called the *rest*. Help children develop their senses of rhythm and their listening skills with this activity.

How to Do It

1. Choose any poem or rhyme that the children enjoy. Say the rhyme for the children.
2. Tell them that you will say it again, and this time, they are to listen for the silence or *rest* between the lines and clap during that rest:

   Roses are red. (Clap)
   Violets are blue. (Clap)
   Sugar is sweet. (Clap)
   And so are you! (Clap)

Expand It!

Repeat the exercise, but instead of clapping, have the children jump!

If You Hear It, Clap!

Help children build their listening skills as they identify the repeated word throughout a rhyme.

How to Do It

1. Choose a poem or rhyme with a repeated word. Recite the poem for the children. Tell children which word to clap on every time they hear it.

   Polly *put the kettle on*
   Polly *put the kettle on*
   Polly *put the kettle on*
   We'll all have tea.
   Sukey *take it off again*
   Sukey *take it off again*
   Sukey *take it off again*
   They've all gone away.

2. Say the rhyme again, and this time, have the children clap on a different word. In our example, the children could listen for *kettle* and *off*.

Expand It!

Instead of clapping, encourage the children to jump or hop on the word.

Move on the Word

Children learn to listen for specific words through this freeze-unfreeze activity.

How to Do It

1. Choose a poem or song, such as "Hot Cross Buns" or "This Little Piggy Went to Market," that contains a repeated word. Teach the poem to the children.
2. Tell the children the word to listen for as you say the poem together. They are to freeze in place as they say the poem and then move only on the chosen word.

    Hot cross **buns** (On *buns*, the children jump or take a giant step.)

    Hot cross **buns**

    One a penny

    Two a penny

    Hot cross **buns**.

    For "This Little Piggy," the children could make a silly piggy face and put their hands up like ears when they hear the word *piggy*.

Expand It!

Each child picks her single movement to perform on the repeated word. Sing the song or poem as a class, and allow each child to do his chosen movement.

Bring a Poem to Life

Use movements to support the children's understanding of rhythm.

How to Do It

1. Choose any poem or rhyme, such as "Little Robin Redbreast," that incorporates movements.
2. Choose a few actions that express the theme or main idea of the poem. Teach the children those actions, and let them use them throughout the poem to move continuously. Mime the actions with the children to teach them.

   Little Robin Redbreast (Flap arms like bird wings)

   Sat upon a rail. (Pretend to sit on a rail)

   Niddle, naddle, went his head, (Move head around)

   Wiggle, waggle, went his tail. (Wiggle your tail)

Expand It!

Repeat the poem, this time pausing for a time between lines. Have the children respond freely to the ideas of the poem in between doing the four movements you have taught them.

A Song in Any Language

Encourage the understanding of similarities between different cultures. If you have children in your classroom who speak a language other than English, ask their families if they have any lullabies or children's songs they would like to share.

How to Do It

1. Choose a children's song or lullaby in a language other than English, such as "Duermete, Mi Niño."
2. Teach the children the song, and then teach them the English translation. Explain that these are the same song in two different languages.
3. Make this a physical activity by adding motions as you sing.

   "Duermete, Mi Niño" ("Go to Sleep")

   Duermete, mi nino (or nina) ("Go to sleep, my child;" pretend to rock a baby in your arms)

   Duermete, mi amor ("Go to sleep, my love;" rock back and forth from side to side)

   Duermete, pedazo de mi corazon. ("Go to sleep, little piece of my heart;" pretend to kiss the baby and place her in a crib)

Expand It!

Encourage the children to get up and dance around in a waltz motion while singing the song.

The First Rhyme Song: "Twinkle, Twinkle, Little Star"

Movements reinforce the rhythm and lyrics of a familiar song.

How to Do It

1. Choose a simple song to sing with the children, such as "Twinkle, Twinkle, Little Star." Sit in circle time and sing the song first, just having children use simple hand motions to illustrate the lyrics.

2. Once they are familiar with the song, ask the children to stand up and sing the song, and have them add these motions:

    Twinkle, twinkle little star, (wiggle fingers while dancing around)
    How I wonder what you are. (open arms wide and look around)
    Up above the world so high (dance while raising arms, wiggle fingers)
    Like a diamond in the sky. (make a diamond shape with hands high in air)
    Twinkle, twinkle little star, (wiggle fingers while dancing around)
    How I wonder what you are. (open arms wide and look around)

3. Now add another fun movement. Say, "The stars are spinning!" Spin around and around in one direction.

4. Say, "Stars, stop! Now go the other way!" Stop and spin around and around in the other direction. (Changing direction keeps kids calm and stops them from getting dizzy.)

Expand It!

Children can be different kinds of stars: fast, slow, spinning slowly, spinning fast, twinkling a little, twinkling a lot, twinkling high, twinkling low, feeling heavy, or feeling light. Children can sit in a circle, and each child can take a turn being the star while standing in the middle while the others sing the song using only hand motions or tapping the rhythm on their knees.

Make It Real

Actions help children recognize the rhythm of a poem or rhyme and make the poem real and vivid.

How to Do It

The following are a few ideas of poems you can act out with the children.

Grey Squirrel

Grey squirrel, grey squirrel, (Jump two times)

Swish your bushy tail. (Shake and wiggle tail)

Grey squirrel, grey squirrel, (Jump two times)

Swish your bushy tail. (Shake and wiggle tail)

Wrinkle up your little nose, (Wiggle nose)

Put a nut between your toes. (Pretend to place a nut between feet)

Grey Squirrel, grey squirrel, (Jump two times)

Swish your bushy tail. (Shake and wiggle tail)

Then children jump around, pretending to be squirrels gathering nuts. You can repeat with each child taking a turn leading the class in a line as the squirrel.

Apple Tree Rhyme

Way up high in the apple tree (Pretend to climb tree, knees high)

Two little apples were smiling at me. (Pretend to hold an apple in each hand and smile)

I shook that apple tree as hard as I could. (Put hands together and shake that tree)

Down came the apples. (Reach up high and show apples falling down)

Mmm! Were they good! (Pretend to hold an apple and eat it. Rub tummy.)

Pretend to pick some more apples at many trees around the room.

This can also be done as snowflakes: *"Way up high in the snowy tree, lots of little snowflakes smiled at me. I shook that tree as hard as I could. Down came the snowflakes. Brrr! They were cold!"*

My Kite Is Up So High

(Sung to the tune of "The Farmer in the Dell")

My kite is up so high! (Pretend to be a kite flying high in the sky)

My kite is up so high!

Oh, me! Oh my! Oh, me! Oh my! Just watch it fly! (Pretend to hold a kite string and fly a kite high in the sky)

Encourage the children to pretend to fly the kites all around the room, fast and slow, high and low. Pretend to be the wind blowing the kites. You can repeat with each child taking a turn leading a line of children that flies one giant kite.

Hickory Dickory Dock

In this activity, children can learn a rhyme with full body movements.

How to Do It

Hickory Dickory Dock (Children make a circle with arms over head for clock, then crouch quickly down to the floor.)

The mouse ran up the clock (Stand up and "run" hands up the body like a little mouse.)

The clock struck one, ding! (Hold up the index finger.)

The mouse ran down (Hands "run" back down the body like the mouse running down the clock.)

Hickory Dickory Dock (Make a circle with arms over head.)

Tick Tock ! (Go up on tiptoes and down.)

Butterflies and Birds

Use any poem about butterflies or birds to reinforce the understanding of prepositions and repetition.

How to Do It

Choose a poem to act out with the children, such as "Butterfly, Butterfly" by Jan Warren or "Once I Saw a Little Bird," a traditional nursery rhyme:

> *Once I saw a little bird* (Children squat down)
>
> *Come hop, hop, hop;* (Stand up and hop on one foot or jump three times)
>
> *So I cried, "Little bird,*
>
> *Will you stop, stop, stop?"* (Freeze in place)
>
> *And was going to the window*
>
> *To say, "How do you do?"* (Pretend to look for the bird)
>
> *But he shook his little tail,* (Shake those tail feathers)
>
> *And far way he flew.* (Pretend to fly around, arms outstretched)

I Am Me

Support children's emotional health and awareness with this fun, rhythmic poem.

How to Do It

1. Ask the children to sit in a circle, and teach them the following poem:

   I feel happy (Stand with two hands on cheeks and a happy face and then arms wide out to the sides)

   I feel sad (Bring hands back to cheeks with a sad face, and crouch down low)

   I feel good (Stand up, touch hands to heart and then arms wide out to the sides)

   I feel bad (Bring hands back in and crouch down low)

   I feel silly (Stand up and make silly waving motions with arms to the sides)

   I fly free (Flap arms as if flying)

   I feel fine (Arms wide out to the sides)

   I AM ME! (Hug self)

2. Ask for volunteers to take turns standing in the middle of the circle and reciting the poem while doing the actions. The group members accompany by tapping the rhythm of the poem on their knees.

Opposites Poem

Use this poem to reinforce the understanding of opposites.

How to Do It

Teach the poem to the children. Do it slowly, starting with the first stanza and then building to the second stanza.

Stop and Go (Freeze, then run in place)

Fast and Slow (Wave hands and arms quickly from low to high. Wave hands and arms slowly from high to low.)

High and Low (Jump up high with arms over head. Crouch down low with hands on the ground.)

Yes and No! (Nod head yes; shake head no.)

What are opposites? (Clap, clap.)

These are opposites! (Hands on hips)

Big and small (Jump, throwing arms and legs open into big X shape. Stretch! Then cup hands together and look inside)

Short and tall (Put palm facing down next to your body at hips or knees. Put palm facing down high above your head to measure tall.)

Straight and round (Stand up straight, then make a circle with arms)

Sky and ground (Stretch up to the sky, then squat)

What are opposites? (Clap, clap.)

These are opposites! (Hands on hips)

Stop and Go (Repeat the motions from above for these four.)

Fast and Slow

High and Low

Yes and No!

Move with Math

The math section provides active lessons so children are on their feet experiencing math concepts, starting from the perspective and orientation of their own bodies. Math learning begins with basic quantitative concepts and extends progressively through number sense, one-to-one correspondence and counting, constructing sets, operations, geometric shapes, patterns and seriation, prediction, and spatial relations.

Little and Big

Support the understanding of the concepts of little and big.

How to Do It

1. Explain to the children they will be little and then they will be big. Ask them to make the shape of a little ball with their hands. (Emphasize the word *little.*)

2. Show the children how to widen their hands to make the imaginary ball a little bigger, then a little bigger, again a little bigger, until their hands reach wide and the ball is really big. (Emphasize the word *big*.)

3. Repeat the exercise, using the shape of a box instead. To show smallest and biggest, have the children make the box the smallest they can and then grow it until their arms are the widest they can reach to make the biggest box.

4. Next, explain to the children that they will pretend to be a big child and then a little baby.

5. Ask the children to be big children by standing tall and running, jumping, and walking with big steps.

6. Then ask the children to be little babies by getting small and rolling, crawling, and walking with little movements.

7. Ask the children to show you how the biggest child and the smallest child would run or crawl.

Long and Short

Support the understanding of the concepts of long and short.

How to Do It

1. Ask the children to lie flat on their tummies on the floor. Ask them to pretend to be a caterpillar, making their bodies long and short repeatedly as they travel from one side of the room to the other.
2. Ask the children to lie flat on their backs and make their bodies the longest they can, and then ask them to scrunch up and make their bodies the shortest they can.
3. Ask the children to sit with knees bent close to their bodies. Ask them to stretch their legs out in front of them, making them long, and then ask them to bend their knees again to make their legs short. Repeat several times.

High and Low

Children reach up high in the sky and touch the clouds, and then they reach down low and touch the ground.

How to Do It

1. Ask the children to pretend to become birds flying high in the sky. Reach the highest in the sky children can reach.
2. Ask them to pretend to be snakes wriggling low on the ground. Go the lowest to the ground the children can go.
3. Ask the children to crouch down in a line at one wall. Tell them that that is a low position. Then, ask them to run to the middle of the room and jump high, and then continue to the other end of the room and jump the highest. Emphasize the words *low, high,* and *highest.*

Wide and Narrow

Do these activities with the children to support understanding of the concepts of wide and narrow.

How to Do It

1. Ask the children stand and make their arms get wide straight out at their sides. Emphasize the word *wide*.
2. Then ask them to make their arms narrow by dropping them to their sides close to their bodies. Emphasize the word *narrow*.
3. Ask the children to take a step to the side to make their legs wide and then step in with the other foot to the side to make their legs narrow.
4. Have children open their legs and arms the widest they can and then close their legs and put arms at their sides to make themselves the narrowest they can.
5. Ask the children to stand on one side of the room and make a wide then narrow pattern as they move to the other side:
   - Step wide with arms wide
   - Step narrow with arms narrow

   Have the children repeat this until they have reached the other side of the room.
6. Ask the children to jump with their legs and arms open wide and then jump bringing in their legs and arms in a narrow position. Go faster and turn the motion into jumping jacks. Ask the children to repeat the word *wide* each time as they open and *narrow* as they close.

Tall and Short

Have fun with the children, pretending to be so tall and so short!

How to Do It

1. Ask the children to think of the tallest tree they can imagine. Then, ask them to pretend to be a tiny seedling for that tree, just starting to grow out of the ground. Encourage them to start by being short, crouched down on the floor. Emphasize the word *short*.

2. Ask them to pretend to grow tall and taller, becoming that tallest tree. As they grow, tell them they are *tall, taller, even taller,* and finally *tallest*.

3. Repeat a few times, letting the children pretend to grow from tiny, short seedlings to tall trees.

Roll Over

Children will enjoy singing this song as they pretend to fall out of bed.

How to Do It

1. Teach the children the lyrics to the song "Roll Over."
   There were ten in a bed, and the little one said,
   "Roll over, roll over"
   So they all rolled over and one fell out.

   There were nine in a bed, and the little one said,
   "Roll over, roll over"
   So they all rolled over and one fell out.
   (continue all the way down to one)
   There was one in a bed, and the little one said,
   "I'm lonely."

2. When the children are comfortable singing the song, ask them to lie down in a line, shoulder to shoulder. Explain that they will pretend they are sleeping in a big bed, just like in the song "Roll Over."

3. Identify the child first in line and the child last in line. The children in between are in the middle of the line.

4. Ask the children to slowly log roll a few times. Then ask the children to freeze, and the child first in line will "fall out" of the bed and run around to get back in the bed and become the last in line.

5. Ask them to start rolling again, continuing in the pattern until each child has had a turn being first and last.

Expand It!

As you sing this song, you can make it a counting and subtraction game. Ask 10 volunteers to stand in a line and act the song out as the whole class sings, with one child sitting down after each verse until only one child is left.

A Few and More and Many

This activity supports children's understanding of creating sets and adding to sets.

How to Do It

1. Ask the children to sit in a line. Explain that they will be coming up to do a freeze dance.

2. Ask for three volunteers to come up and dance. Play some music and let them dance for a moment; then say, "Freeze!" Explain that there are a *few* children who are dancing. A *few* means just three or four.

3. Ask for a few more volunteers, and start the dancing again. After a few moments, say "Freeze!" Explain that there are *more* children dancing.

4. Ask the rest of the children to join the dancers. After a few moments, say, "Freeze!" Tell the children that there are *many* children dancing.

Expand It!

To add the element of subtracting from a set, continue the activity, subtracting each time you freeze the dancers. Tell the children that there are many, then fewer, then even fewer children dancing. Be sure to emphasize the words *many* or *fewer* each time you freeze and subtract from the group.

One and a Group

Encourage understanding of the concepts of one and a group or set.

How to Do It

1. Ask the children to stand scattered around the room, with arms out to the side so each has her own space.
2. Ask them to look around, and explain they are now standing alone, *one* person in each place.
3. Ask the children to come together, making a circle and holding hands in the middle of the room. Explain that now they are all together, as a *group* or *set*.
4. Continuing to hold hands, move around in a circle first one way and then the other direction. Explain that you are moving as a *group* or *a set*.
5. Ask the children to leave the circle and go back to their original spots, one person in each spot.

Early and Late

Reinforce children's understanding of sequences and patterns.

How to Do It

1. Ask the children to lie down on the floor. Tell them they will pretend it is morning time and they will pretend to wake up.

2. Say, "What time of day is it? It is morning. It is early in the day. What do we do early in the day?" Listen to suggestions from the children.

3. Say, "Early in the day, we get up, get dressed, and eat breakfast! Let's pretend to do those things." Encourage the children to pretend to get up, get dressed, and eat breakfast.

4. Ask, "What do we do much later?" Listen to the suggestions from the children. Guide them to a discussion of things they do at nighttime. "Late in the day we have dinner, take a bath, read a bedtime story, and go to sleep. Let's pretend to do those things." Encourage the children to pretend to eat dinner, take a bath, read a story, and go to sleep.

Counting in Books

Use this fun activity to expand any book that focuses on counting and number recognition.

How to Do It

1. Choose a book that incorporates counting, such as *Big Fat Hen* by Keith Baker or *Counting Crocodiles* by Judy Sierra. Read the book with the children.

2. Read the book a second time, and ask the children to stand up and act out the story:

   One, two, buckle my shoe (Children say *one, two,* then pretend to put on shoe)

   Three, four, shut the door (Children say *three, four,* then pretend to shut a door)

   Five, six, pick up sticks. (Children say *five, six,* then pretend to pick up sticks)

3. Continue through the book, encouraging the children to say the numbers with you as you read.

One-to-One Correspondence

Help children grasp the concept of one-to-one correspondence by using their bodies to show the numbers found in a favorite book.

How to Do It

1. Choose a book to read to the children that focuses on counting skills, such as *Chicka Chicka Boom Boom* by John Archambault and Bill Martin Jr.; *1, 2, 3 to the Zoo* by Eric Carle; *One Was Johnny* by Maurice Sendak; *Quack and Count* by Keith Baker; or *How Do Dinosaurs Count to 10?* by Jane Yolen.

2. As you read, encourage the children to take turns standing up to show the number of things (animals, objects, people) represented by the numbers. For example, as you read *1, 2, 3 to the Zoo* by Eric Carle, tell the children that the train-car beds will be in the space in front of them, between your reading chair and the area where they are seated. Then, the children can act out each animal in turn:

   ● One elephant—One child stands up and becomes an elephant, moving and sounding like an elephant, and then that child stands (or sits) on the train car.

   ● Two hippos—Two more children stand up and become hippos, moving and sounding like hippos, and then stand (or sit) on the train car next to the one elephant.

   ● Three giraffes—Three more children stand up and become giraffes, moving and sounding like giraffes, then standing (or sitting) on the third train care next to the two hippos.

3. Continue through the book. When the number of animals becomes higher than the number of children in the class, have the children who acted out the smaller numbers leave their train car and become the higher numbers on new train cars. Or, you may choose to act out parts of the book and simply read the rest.

Bunny Hop Counting

Learn to count to five using a fun bunny hop!

How to Do It

1. Tell the children that they will pretend to be bunnies, hopping across the room. Ask them to line up at the wall and face the opposite wall.

2. Start with the number one, and ask the children to take one bunny hop as they call out, "One!"

3. Ask them to continue taking one hop at a time, calling out, "One!" until they reach the other side of the room.

4. Ask them to turn around and take two bunny hops, calling out, "One, two!" as they hop. Encourage them to hop, calling out, "One, two," until they get to the other side of the room.

5. Continue in this way through five bunny hops. When they have crossed the room five bunny hops at a time, ask them to take a well-earned bunny rest! Whew!

Expand It!

Ask for volunteers to lead the class in counting as they bunny hop around the room. Give each child a turn to lead the line in bunny hopping and counting.

Ones and Twos

Reinforce children's understanding of one-to-one correspondence and the concept of pairs.

How to Do It

1. Ask the children to stand or sit in a line and watch what you do.
2. Identify pairs of body parts, counting them aloud:

     One (Lift one hand. Put hand back down.)

     Two (Lift two hands. Put hands back down.)

     I have one hand. (Lift one hand. Put hand back down.)

     I have two hands. (Lift two hands. Put hands back down.)

     One (Lift one hand. Put hand back down.)

     Two (Lift two hands. Put hands back down.)

     They're a pair. (Shake hands or clap them together)
3. Encourage the children to do the actions with you.
4. Repeat with more body parts: knees, elbows, feet, legs, arms, eyes, ears, and so on.

Expand It!

Move faster through the exercise, creating more of a coordination challenge for the class and creating the opportunity for some laughter and fun learning.

Jumping Jack Fun

This is a fun activity that strengthens coordination and counting skills.

How to Do It

1. Ask the children to stand well spaced around the room.
2. Break the jumping-jack action into two parts: first teach the children to jump and land with their legs wide apart, then to bring their legs back together: When you count number *one,* they are to jump out with their legs apart. When you count the number *two,* they are to bring their feet back together. Practice a few times so they can get the hang of it.
3. Now teach the children to use just their arms. When you count *one,* they are to hold their arms out wide and up high. When you count *two,* they are to being their arms back down to their sides. Practice a few times.
4. Combine the actions, counting as you move:
   One! (Jump out and hold arms out)
   Two! (Close feet and bring hands to sides)

I See One Child; I See Two

Support children's understanding of one-to-one correspondence.

How to Do It

1. Ask the children to sit with you on the rug. Tell them that you are going to say a counting poem.

2. Ask one child to stand up. Say the following:
   I see one child.
   One!
   Say the number with me: One! (The children repeat, "One!")

3. Ask another child to stand up with the first child. Say:
   I see two children.
   Two!
   Say the number with me: Two!

4. Say the following poem, asking the children to join you at the end:
   I see one child!
   I see two!
   We'll do a one-two dance with you!
   One! Two! One! Two! (Encourage the standing children to stomp their feet, 1-2, 1-2 The seated children can stomp their feet while sitting.)

5. Ask the first two children to sit down. Call up another child, and continue as before, until all of the children have had a turn to stand up and dance. If your class has an odd number of children, use a stuffed animal or toy as the "second child" in the last pair.

6. At the end, have all children get up and dance together.

Expand It!

Continue to add children and count to three, four, or five. If your students are comfortable with counting up to five, extend the activity to count up to 10. Just change the third line of the poem to "We'll do a stomping dance with you!"

1, 2, 3—Arms, Tap, Knee

Support understanding of sequence and one-to-one correspondence.

How to Do It

1. Ask the children to sit in a large circle, and teach them the following actions: arms up overhead, hands tap tummy, squat down and place hands and knees on the floor.
2. Once they are comfortable with the actions, teach them the chant, *1, 2, 3—Arms, Tap, Knee.*
3. Say the chant and do the actions together.
4. Invite the children to take turns walking around the circle, while the class chants, "One, two, three, one, two, three." When the child returns to his spot, he will do the actions, arms, tap, knee, and have a seat.

Ride Your Bicycle

Reinforce counting to three while encouraging physical fitness.

How to Do It

1. Invite the children to sit in a circle. Tell them you are going to pretend to ride on imaginary bicycles.

2. Ask them to lean back, with their feet in the air. Tell them to pedal their feet as if they are riding a bike.

3. Next, tell them that you will take an imaginary ride. "Get on your bicycles! It's a beautiful day, and it's time to ride! Hand, hand" (the children place a hand on each imaginary handlebar), "foot, foot" (the children press each imaginary pedal). "Hand, hand, foot, foot."

4. Encourage the children to pretend to ride. "Ready to ride?" Rhythmically repeat: "Ride and ride and ride and ride!"

5. Ask, "How many birds do we see? Let's count!" (Count to three.) "Keep pedaling."

6. Continue, asking how many dogs or cats or cars you see. Each time, count to three.

7. Tell the children that you are back at school, and it's time to get off their bicycles. Say, "Get off your bicycles! Let's count to three and stand up. One, two, three! Up!"

I Do; You Do

This is a game and chant of counting up to one, two, three, four.

How to Do It

1. Invite the children to stand in a line, and teach them the following chant:

   I do, you do (Point to self, then point to the children)

   1, 2, 1, 2 (Clap on the beat)

   What I do, (Point to self)

   You do, too! (Point to the children)

   1, 2, 3, 1, 2, 3 (Clap on the beat)

   When I do this, (Point to self)

   You do it, too! (Point to the children)

   1, 2, 3, 4, 1, 2, 3, 4 (Clap on the beat)

2. Repeat until the children get the hang of it. Then, change the actions; for example, tap, stomp, pump arm, shake head, and open and close fingers.

Dinosaur March and Count

This activity can be done anywhere: in the hall, outside on the playground, or in the classroom.

How to Do It

1. Teach the children the following chant:

   One, two, three, four!
   We will march like dinosaurs!
   One, two, three, four!
   We will roar like dinosaurs!
   Roar!

2. Ask the children to stand in a line. Ask the child who is the class line leader for the week to lead the march.

Expand It!

Divide the class into two even groups. Form two lines, and have two lines face each other. They can march in place and chant as they watch each other. This is sure to bring on some giggles.

1, 2, 3, 4: Hip, Hop, Move!

Use a Caribbean-inspired dance to help children understand counting to four.

How to Do It

1. Ask the children to stand in a circle. Teach them the following chant:

   1, 2, 3, 4

   1, 2, 3, 4

   1, 2, 3, 4

   Hip, Hop, Move!

2. Teach the children the actions, slowly at first:

   Twist, twist, twist, stomp.

   Twist, twist, twist, stomp.

   Twist, twist, twist, twist.

   Hip—push out hip to left

   Hop—push out hip to right

   Move—small jump to the side,

      landing on both feet.

3. Repeat the actions several
   times, and then add the
   chant. Younger children
   can just shimmy or wiggle
   to the rhythm while counting; older children
   will be more precise in their actions.

Counting Steps

Use this activity while waiting in line, walking down the hall, or anytime to strengthen counting skills, coordination, and cross-body patterning.

How to Do It

1. Ask the children to stand in a line.
2. Teach the children the following movements, counting out loud to four for each movement:
   - Stamp feet four times.
   - Clap hands four times.
   - Brush off right shoulder four times.
   - Brush off left shoulder four times.
   - Stamp feet four times.
   - Clap hands four times.
   - Punch right arm in the air toward the left shoulder.
   - Punch left arm in the air toward the right shoulder.

Expand It!

Ask the children to form two lines and face each other. As they do the exercise, tell them to clap the hands of their partner in front of them.

Count to Five

Reinforce the children's understanding of counting and one-to-one correspondence.

How to Do It

1. Lead the children in the following motions:
   Tap head, tap shoulders, touch knees, touch toes, hands on floor with feet out behind into a pushup position, back to a squat, touch toes, touch knees, stand and tap shoulders, tap head. Practice a few times until the children are comfortable with the movements.

2. Add counting to the movements:
   Tap head—one
   Tap shoulders—two
   Touch knees—three
   Touch toes—four
   Pushup position—five
   Jump back into squat—one
   Touch toes—two
   Touch knees—three
   Stand and tap shoulders—four
   Tap head—five

Expand It!

Play some lively music and encourage the children to do the movements to the beat.

Tap Dance Counting

To make counting fun, the children can use their hands and feet to make noise while counting out loud.

How to Do It

1. Ask the children to stand in a line with their hands on their hips. Count together out loud: "one, two, three, four, five, six." Repeat the counting a few times until they are comfortable counting to six.

2. Next, teach them the following motions:
   - Stand with the weight on the left foot, right foot out.
   - Tap the toes on the right foot three times.
   - Stand with the weight on the right foot, left foot out.
   - Tap the toes on the left foot three times.
   - Jump three times.
   - Clap three times.

3. Now, put it all together:

   Put your hands on your hips! (Children place hands on hips)

   Stand on one foot (Pick up the right foot, balancing on the left foot)

   Tap your toes on the floor: 1, 2, 3 (Tap right toes on the floor to the beat, counting aloud one, two, three)

   Let's do the other foot!

   Stand on one foot (Pick up the left foot, balancing on the right foot)

   Tap your toes on the floor: 4, 5, 6 (Tap the left toes on the floor to the beat, counting aloud four, five, six)

   Let's do that again! (Repeat actions)

   Now we'll use both feet!

   Jump on two feet: 1, 2, 3 (Jump up and down, count one, two, three)

   Clap your hands: 4, 5, 6 (Clap and count four, five, six)

   Do it again! (Repeat actions)

   Let's put it all together!

   Tap one foot: 1, 2, 3 (Tap the right toes on the floor to the beat, count one, two, three)

   Tap the other foot: 4, 5, 6 (Tap the left toes on floor to the beat, count four, five, six)

   Jump: 1, 2, 3 (Jump up and down, count one, two, three)

   Clap: 4, 5, 6 (Clap your hands, count four, five, six)

Expand It!

Encourage the children to find partners and face each other. Do the exercise mirroring each other. Instead of children clapping with their own hands, have them clap their partner's hands.

Counting Cheer

Children will enjoy this loud activity!

How to Do It

1. Gather the children together and teach them the following cheer:

   One, two, three, four!

   Who you gonna cheer for?

   Our class!

   Our class!

   Yay, our class!

   Five, six, seven, eight!

   Who do you think is really great?

   Our class!

   Our class!

   Yay, our class!

2. Now add motions:

   One, two, three, four!

   Who you gonna cheer for? (Children tap hands on legs)

   Our class! (Fist up in air)

   Our class! (Other fist up in air)

   Yay, our class! (Crouch down, then jump high)

   Five, six, seven, eight!

   Who do you think is really great? (Repeat actions)

   Our class!

   Our class!

   Yay, our class!

Expand It!

Use this to cheer for another class at your school or center or as a thank you for someone who has helped your class.

One Little, Two Little, Three Little— Counting to Nine

Encourage counting from one to nine and the understanding of number order.

How to Do It

1. Gather the children to sit with you, and teach them the following song to the tune of "One Little, Two Little, Three Little Indians":

   One little, two little, three little bouncy knees. (Bounce knees up and down.)
   Four little, five little, six little bouncy knees.
   Seven little, eight little, nine little bouncy knees.
   Every day we move around!

2. Repeat, changing the motions each time:
   - Stomping feet
   - Pumping fists
   - Jumping feet
   - Shrugging shoulders
   - Nodding heads
   - Shaking hands

To the Count of Ten

Children will enjoy anticipating the freeze on the count of 10.

How to Do It

1. Ask the children to stand in the center of the room. Tell them that you will call out an action and they will have until the count of 10 to complete that action. When you reach the number 10, they will freeze.

2. Practice counting slowly from one to ten with the children, to give them a sense of how long that is.

3. Begin with a simple action, such as moving from one side of the room to the other. Tell the children, "You have until the count of 10 to walk to the other side of the room! Count with me. One, two, three, four, five, six, seven, eight, nine, ten! Freeze!"

4. Ask the children to look around and see all the different poses in which their classmates are frozen. Tell them, "Okay, unfreeze!"

4. Try this activity using a variety of different actions:
   - Spin around one way.
   - Spin around the other way.
   - Pretend to put on your shirt and pants.
   - Pretend to brush your teeth.
   - Grow from a crawling baby into a walking child.
   - Wiggle.
   - Jump up and down.

Lizard-Walk Fives

For children who are already comfortable with counting, introduce the concept of counting by fives.

How to Do It

1. Gather the children and ask them to hold up their hands. Ask them how many fingers they have on one hand.
2. All together, count the five fingers on one hand, and then count the five fingers on the other hand.
3. Teach children the pattern of skip-counting by fives. Encourage them to hold up each hand in turn as they count by fives: 5, 10, 15, 20, 25, and so on.
4. Once the children have begun to be comfortable with counting by fives, tell them they will pretend to be lizards. Lizards can walk on the ground or up a wall or even up a tree trunk.
5. Ask them to pretend to walk like lizards, moving one hand at a time very slowly. (Feet, too, but concentrate on the hands for counting in this exercise.) Try walking like lizards, around on the floor, with their hands up against a real wall.
6. Add counting by fives as they walk. Count together as they make each hand motion.

Frog-Jump Tens

For children who are comfortable with counting, introduce the concept of counting by tens.

How to Do It

1. Ask the children to sit with knees bent and to look at their feet.
2. All together, count the five toes on one foot and then the five toes on the other foot. Tell the children that five toes plus five toes makes ten toes. Count to 10 together.
3. Teach children the pattern of skip-counting by tens: 10, 20, 30, 40, and so on. Keep a slow, even beat.
4. Tell children they will pretend to be frogs. As the children jump like frogs, they will be able see their feet when they land, if they look down at them. Their 10 toes will land on the floor.
5. Encourage the children to try jumping like frogs. Ask them to notice their feet when they land.
6. Add the counting to the frog jumping. Count all together. For each jump, count by tens. Encourage the children to "ribbet" between jumps if they wish.

Measuring with Hands

Practice measuring and counting with nonstandard units.

How to Do It

1. Ask the children to line up on one side of the room.
2. Ask them how many hands they think it would take to measure all the way across the room. Listen to their ideas. How many hands to get to the rug? How many hands to measure across the table?
3. Get down on hands and knees with the children and demonstrate how to measure using just your hands as the unit of measure.
4. Measure a short distance with the children, counting out loud together up to 10 while the children walk on all fours to the beat of the count—each hand placement is one beat.
5. Ask the children to stand up and see how far they traveled in 10 handprints.
6. Vary the game by measuring different objects in the classroom with hands as the unit of measurement:
   - Wall
   - Bulletin board
   - Table
   - Rug
   - Door
   - Window
   - Line of tape
   - Their own leg
   - A friend's leg

Expand It!

Measure objects in the room using the children's feet as the nonstandard unit. Show them how to measure by walking toe to heel.

Counting Clock

Support the children's understanding of time in a day and time on a clock.

How to Do It

1. Show the children an analog clock (the kind with a face and hands). Point out that the clock is a circle with numbers on it. Show them the numbers 1 through 12, counting as you move the hands around. Children do not need to be able to count to 12 themselves to understand the idea of this exercise.

2. Move the hands around again, this time mentioning the progression in times of day: getting up in the morning, eating breakfast, coming to school, eating lunch, learning time, home, dinnertime, bath, story, and bedtime.

3. Ask the children to stand in a circle. Tell them they will each be a clock. They are standing in a circle because clocks go in circles.

4. Have children raise both arms high over their heads. Their arms and hands will be the "hands" of the clock. They start with arms up high at 12 o'clock on their clocks.

5. Encourage the children to imitate your movements as you count from 1 to 12 while moving your arms like the movement of a clock: "tick, tick, tick" and move your hands together, using both arms at the same time around in the circle of the clock.

6. After one rotation, say "Ding! The sun is up, and you are awake! Let's do some jumping jacks! Let's count while we jump. One, two, three, four, five, six, seven, eight, nine, ten, eleven, twelve!"

7. Repeat the motion of the clock arms, counting up to 12. Say, "Ding! The sun is down, and you are asleep! Lie down and go to sleep! Let's count while we sleep." Count to 12.

8. Repeat as long as the children are interested, or change the time of day to dinnertime (pretend to eat) or playtime (dance around) or bathtime (pretend to take a bath).

A Counting Adventure

Make up a story and count as you act it out.

How to Do It

1. Tell the children that you are going on an adventure together. The story can be about anything. For our example, we will go on a treasure hunt. Tell the children, "It's time to go on an adventure, a treasure-hunt adventure! Put on your hiking shoes and your hat; we're going to the jungle!" Encourage the children to pretend to put on their shoes and hats and walk to the jungle.

2. When you have arrived, encourage the children to look around and pretend to see all sorts of jungle creatures. Ask them to pretend to take their treasure maps out of their pockets. "Open your treasure maps! Wow, there are 10 clues on this map! Can you count them with me?" Use one hand to point at the other and count up to 10 as a class.

3. "Read" your treasure map: "The first clue says, 'Find one big tree!' I see a big tree. One tree!" (Pretend to see a tree.) "The second clue says, 'Find two vines.' I see some vines hanging here! Let's count. One. Two. Let's swing from these vines to get to that hill over there." (The children swing arms two times, as if swinging from a vine.)

4. Continue in this manner, pretending to read the treasure map, counting the clues, and acting out the adventure:

   - Take three giant steps to get to a cave. Pretend to crawl inside the cave.
   - You hear four bats flying around. Count the bats as you duck to avoid them.
   - You leave the cave and see a stream. Step on five stones to cross the stream.
   - You see six turtles sunning themselves on a log by the stream. Count the turtles, pretending to hide inside shells like turtles do.
   - While pretending to be turtles, the adventurers fall asleep! Pretend to sleep on the floor.
   - When you wake up, it is dark and all the sounds in the jungle have changed. You hear a cricket chirp seven times.
   - The sun comes up, and you start walking again. You see eight gorillas, who point you in the direction you should go.
   - You come to a long bridge. It will take nine steps to cross the bridge.

- Pull out your treasure maps again. Remind the children of the clues you have found so far: one tree, two vines, three giant steps to the cave, four bats, five stones to cross the stream, six turtles, seven chirps from a cricket, eight gorillas, nine steps to cross the bridge. What's next? Ten!

- Clue number 10 says that the sun will shine in the spot where the treasure lies! Encourage the children to look around the room for the spot where the sun is shining and to point to it.

- The treasure rests at the bottom of a hill. Encourage the children to lie down on one side of the room and log-roll together in the same direction, 10 times.

- Bump! The children bump into the treasure chest. Pretend to open the chest.

- Ask the children to take turns telling you what is inside. Pretend to take out each item.

Number Search

Reinforce numeral recognition with this fun twist on a scavenger hunt.

How to Do It

Before beginning, trace numerals on heavy paper and cut them out. Make several (three or four) of each numeral. For older children, make 0 through 9; for younger children, start with 1 through 4 or just make several of the number they are learning. Scatter the numerals around the room.

1. Gather the children to sit with you, and tell them there are numbers all around. Tell them you know that you have seen a number 1 (hold up a 1 and remind them of what it looks like). Continue, naming the numerals and showing the examples of the numerals you have placed around the room.

2. Ask the children to help you find all of these numbers. Tell them you would like for them to find a numeral that you call out, walk to it, touch it, and then return to the rug. Remind them to leave the numbers where they are, because you will need them later.

3. Say, "Now, I will call out a number, and I would like for you to find it. Please find a number ___!"

4. Encourage the children to look for and touch the appropriate numeral, then return to the rug. Repeat with all the numbers.

5. When the children have discovered all the numerals, add an action to do while finding the numbers; for example, "Let's try galloping to find the number ___." Repeat to find all of the numerals. Suggestions: floating, flying, marching, and swimming.

Count with Thumbkin

Learn one-to-one correspondence through identification of numbers of body parts.

How to Do It

1. Teach the children the song "Where Is Thumbkin?"

   Where is Thumbkin? (Start with hands behind back)

   Where is Thumbkin?

   Here I am. (Bring right hand to front, with thumb up)

   Here I am. (Bring left hand to front, with thumb up)

   How are you this morning?

   Very well, I thank you. (Wiggle thumbs as if they're talking to each other)

   Run away. (Hide right hand behind back)

   Run away. (Hide left hand behind back)

   Where is pointer?

   Where is pointer?

   Here I am. (Bring right hand to front, with index finger up)

   Here I am. (Bring left hand to front, with index finger up)

   How are you this morning?

   Very well, I thank you. (Wiggle fingers as if they're talking to each other)

   Run away. (Hide right hand behind back)

   Run away. (Hide left hand behind back)

   Continue with each finger: tall man (middle finger), ring man (fourth finger), and pinkie, then the family (whole hands).

2. Talk about the parts of their bodies that come in twos, such as hands, eyes, ears, and feet. If there is a child in your class who has special needs, then adjust the song to include something that child has two of—perhaps wheels.

3. Sing the "Where Is Thumbkin?" song again, this time singing about the pairs of body parts:

 I have one hand, (Hold up right hand)
 I have one hand.
 I have two, I have two. (Hold up left hand to join it)
 How are you today sir? (One hand "talks" to the other)
 Very fine, I thank you. (Other hand "answers.")
 Run away! Run away! (Hands hide behind back)
 Continue singing about the eyes, ears, feet, or legs.

One Is Foot and Two Is Hand

Using the tune of "The Alphabet Song," help children learn the order of the numbers, one through nine.

How to Do It

1. Sing the following song to the tune of "The Alphabet Song." Sing the song slowly, so the children can follow your actions.

   One is foot, (Point to foot)

   And two is hand. (Hold up hand)

   Three is hips, (Hand on hip)

   and now we jam! (Shake upper body)

   (Pause)

   One is hand, (Hold up hand)

   And two is knees. (Point to knees)

   Three is fingers. (Hold up fingers)

   Bend down, please. (Bend upper body down and back up)

   (Pause)

   Four is elbows, (Move elbows)

   And five is head. (Point to head)

   Six is wiggle. (Wiggle upper body)

   Now, jump instead! (Jump)

   (Pause)

   Seven is shoulders, (Point to shoulders)

   and eight is knees. (Point to knees)

   Nine is fingers. (Hold up fingers)

   Sit down, please! (Sit down)

2. Sing this song any time the children have to wait in line for a few moments, or as a way to help them focus after a more active period.

Coming 'Round the Mountain

Help children understand the concept of adding to and taking away from sets.

How to Do It

1. Ask the children to sit in a circle. Sing the following song while seated, so the children can learn the words first:

   One is coming 'round the mountain when he (or she) comes.

   One is coming 'round the mountain when he comes.

   One is coming 'round the mountain,

   One is coming 'round the mountain,

   One is coming 'round the mountain when he comes.

   Add one!

   Two are coming 'round the mountain when they come. (Continue singing about two)

   Add one!

   Three are coming 'round the mountain when they come. (Continue singing about three)

   Add one!

   Four are coming 'round the mountain when they come. (Continue singing about four)

   Add one!

   Five are coming 'round the mountain when they come. (Continue singing about five)

2. Now tell the children that they will act out the song, beginning with one child and adding a child for each verse. Tell the children they will gallop around the circle as the rest of the class sings.

3. Ask for a volunteer to be the first one. Sing the song again, adding another child to gallop around the circle with each verse.

4. When the song is over, ask the children how many are galloping 'round the mountain.

5. Continue singing, with new gallopers.

Expand It!

When the children are comfortable adding to the set who are galloping around the circle, try subtracting! Start with five and gradually subtract until there is one child left.

When I Was One

Support children's understanding of one-to-one correspondence and number order.

How to Do It

Teach children the following song, to the tune of the folk song "When I Was One."
Sing the numbers up to the age of the children in your class, or go beyond and put the words in future tense.

When I was one,
I wiggled my thumb (Wiggle thumb and body)
Going over the sea. (Make hand motion of boat on water)
I jumped aboard a pirate ship, (Jump)
And the pirate said to me: (Hands on hips)
Going over, going under, (Make hand motions of a boat)
Stand at attention like a soldier, (Stand and salute like a soldier)
With a 1, 2, 3! (Stamp feet three times)

When I was two I put on my shoe. (Mime putting on shoe)
When I was three I climbed a tree. (Mime climbing a tree)
When I was four I shut the door. (Mime shutting a door)
When I was five I jumped and jived! (Jump and move head and body side to side)

Jump Open, Jump Close

Use jumping jacks with claps to support children's understanding of counting to two.

How to Do It

1. Ask the children to spread out, with space around each child.
2. Teach them how to do a jumping jack. Practice several times so they get the hang of it.
3. Tell them you will now say the number one for jumping out and two for jumping feet together.
4. Using just your feet, count "One!" and jump out, with feet apart. Then count, "Two!" and jump, putting feet back together. Repeat several times.
5. Now try just using your arms. Count, "One!" and clap your hands over your head. Then count, "Two!" and bring your arms back down to your sides. Repeat several times.
6. Next, put it all together. Count, "One!" and jump out and clap hands over head. Count, "Two!" and close feet and bring hands to your sides. Repeat several times.

Expand It!

Have children pair up; they can do the exercise together facing each other.

Counting Ones and Twos

Identify the difference between one and two.

How to Do It

1. Ask the children to name a body part that they have only one of; for example, the nose or the mouth. Ask them to name body parts that they have two of; for example, arms, legs, or ears.

2. Sing the following song to the tune of "Let's Say Hello to (Name), How are You?" Tell the children they will count what they have one of on their bodies and what they have two of on their bodies.

   What do we have one of, one of, one of?

   What do we have one of?

   Look, let's see. (Name a few: head, heart, body, bellybutton, mouth, and nose.)

   What do we have two of, two of, two of?

   What do we have two of?

   Look, let's see. (Name a few: eyes, hands, feet, legs, arms, knees, and ears.)

3. Next, add actions to the song:

   What do we have one of, one of, one of? (Hands on hips, bend side to side)

   What do we have one of?

   Look, let's see.

   Head! (Children move their heads)

   Mouth! (Open and close and make silly faces)

   What do we have two of, two of, two of? (Hands on hips, bend side to side)

   What do we have two of?

   Look, let's see.

   Eyes! (Open and close eyes)

   Hands! (Wiggle hands)

   Feet! (Stamp feet)

Yankee Doodle Feather

Act out the song "Yankee Doodle Dandy" as you reinforce understanding of simple addition.

How to Do It

1. Invite the children to stand well spaced in a circle. Sing "Yankee Doodle Dandy" and use these actions to make it a math exercise. Pretend that Yankee Doodle's hat is in the center of the circle.

   Yankee Doodle went to town (March in place)

   A-riding on a pony. (Gallop to center of circle)

   Stuck a feather in his hat (Pretend to place a feather in the imaginary hat; hold up one finger)

   And called it macaroni! (Wiggle backward to the big circle)

2. Repeat the song and movements, increasing the number of feathers each time from two to three and all the way up to five.

3. Encourage the children to gallop around and pretend to be Yankee Doodle with lots of feathers in his cap.

Days of the Week Counting

This activity supports counting, number sequence, and learning the days of the week.

How to Do It

1. Ask the children to sit in a circle. Sing the following song to the tune of "Where Is Thumbkin?" Note: We have started with Monday because it is the beginning of the school week. If you prefer to follow a calendar week, begin with Sunday.

   One is Monday, one is Monday. (Hold up one finger to "talk" to the finger on the other hand)
   Yes, it is; yes, it is.
   How are you on Monday?
   Very well, I thank you.
   One is Monday, one is Monday.

2. Continue through the days of the week. When you get to six and seven, just hold up the appropriate number of fingers.

   Two is Tuesday, two is Tuesday. (Hold up two fingers to "talk" to two fingers on the other hand)
   Yes, it is; yes, it is.
   How are you on Tuesday?
   Very well, I thank you.
   Two is Tuesday, two is Tuesday.

3. Sing the song a few times together. When the children are comfortable with it, sing again, this time pausing to let the children fill in the days of the week. For example, sing, "Two is _____." Pause to let the children say, "Tuesday!"

Expand It!

Encourage volunteers to take turns telling you what day it is today and then leading the class in the song.

Now, Let's Add One!

Reinforce the concept of adding to a set as you sing this silly song to the tune of "Macarena"!

How to Do It

1. Ask the children to sit in a wide half circle or along one wall.

2. Teach the children the following song, sung to the tune of "Macarena." It may be helpful to play the song for the children so they can get the rhythm.

   *I see **one** wiggle all around.* (Emphasize the number)

   I hear her (or him) clap,

   And we touch the ground.

   I see one wiggle all around.

   Now—let's add one! (Ay!)

   *I see **two** wiggle all around.* (Emphasize the number)

   I hear them clap,

   And they touch the ground.

   I see two wiggle all around.

   Now, let's add one! (Ay!)

3. Ask the children to stand up, and tell them you will call on volunteers one at a time to dance to the song. Start the song again, and call one child up to wiggle while the class sings.

4. Continue, calling another child up to join the first. Call up another child each time the class sings, "Now, let's add one!"—adding up to four (or however high the class is able to count).

5. Ask the children who have gotten to wiggle to sit down, and then start over with other children, again adding up to four or as high as you wish to go.

Expand It!

If the children are ready for skip counting, try adding children by twos.

One Foot, Two Feet

Help children understand one-to-one correspondence and a simple A-B pattern.

How to Do It

1. Ask the children to stand in a line on one side of the room.
2. Teach them the following chant:
    One hand, two hands,
    One foot, two feet.
3. Make the pattern clear by speaking this script as the children move and you demonstrate:
    I have one hand. (hold up one hand)
    I have two hands. (hold up both hands)
    I have one foot. (hold out one foot, and take a giant step)
    I have two feet. (take two giant steps; stand with feet together)
4. Repeat this pattern—one hand, two hands, one foot, two feet—from one side of the room to the other side of the room.

And Another One Came!

Children love to wiggle! Combine the movement with learning simple addition.

How to Do It

1. Ask the children to sit in a circle. Ask for a volunteer to come stand in the center of the circle.

2. Give the volunteer an action to do, such as hopping, jumping, clapping, swaying, or making an animal noise.

3. Ask the children, "How many children are (hopping, jumping, clapping)?" Let them answer, "One!" Help them if they need assistance in responding. Say, "I see one child (hopping, jumping, clapping)."

4. Ask the volunteer to freeze. Ask for another volunteer to join the first child in doing the action again. Say, "And another one came!" Let the second child join the first. "Everyone wave and say hello!" Encourage the children to wave. Tell the children, "We had one, and we added one. Now, how many children are (hopping, jumping, clapping)?" Help them answer, "Two!" Say, "Let's count: one, two! One plus one is two!"

5. Ask the two children to freeze. Ask for another volunteer to join the first two in doing the action again. Say, "And another one came!" and let the third child join the other two. "Everyone wave and say hello!" Tell the children, "We had two, and we added one. Now, how many children are (hopping, jumping, clapping)?" Help them answer, "Three!" Say, "Let's count: one, two, three! Two plus one is three!"

6. Continue in this manner, adding as many children to the set as is appropriate for your class. For younger children, stop at three or four. For older children, add as many as you think they are ready to add.

Hand Jive

For children who can already count to ten, try this fun way of learning to count by fives.

How to Do It

1. This exercise only involves the hands and is a fun way to reorganize and focus the group. Students should look at their hands while they do the activity.

2. Teach the children the following song, sung like a musical scale going up and then back down.

   One, two, three, four, five, five, five! (Go up the scale)

   Six, seven, eight, nine, ten, ten, ten! (Go down the scale)

   Five and five

   Is ten, ten, ten!

   Shake it out,

   And do it again!

3. Add hand motions to the song:

   One (Stick out left thumb)

   Two (Open left index finger)

   Three (Left middle finger)

   Four (Left ring finger)

   Five, five, five! (Left pinky finger and pulse left hand two more times)

   Six (Stick out right thumb)

   Seven (Open right index finger)

   Eight (Right middle finger)

   Nine (Right ring finger)

   Ten, ten, ten! (Right pinky finger and pulse right hand two more times)

   Five and five (Pulse left hand and look at it; pulse right hand and look at it)

   Is ten, ten, ten! (Pulse both hands three times while looking at them)

   Shake it out (Shake hands out as if flicking water off hands)

   And do it again! (Close both hands back into fists)

Expand It!

Try moving the pinkies open first. Start with fists that hide the thumb to allow the pinky to start the pattern.

One Goes Away!

Support the children's understanding of subtracting from a set.

How to Do It

1. To help children understand subtracting from a set, begin with a block demonstration. Ask the children to sit with you, and show them two blocks. Count the blocks together: "One, two. There are two blocks."

2. Now, take one block away. Tell the children, "One goes away. Now, how many blocks are there?" Count the block: "One!" Repeat this if necessary to help the children understand.

3. Ask the children to stand in a large circle. Give them an action to do, such as jumping, clapping, swaying, or making an animal noise. Have children practice the action.

4. Ask two volunteers to step forward, and ask the rest of the children to sit. Ask the two volunteers to do the action. Say, "There are two children (jumping, clapping, swaying). Count them with me: one, two!"

5. Ask the two volunteers to freeze. Say, "I see two children. One, two. Now, one goes away." Ask one volunteer to sit down. "Wave bye to this one!"

6. Ask the remaining volunteer to start the action again. Ask the children, "One went away. How many children are left (jumping, clapping, swaying)?" Encourage the children to answer, "One!" Say, "We had two children here. When one goes away, one child is still here. One. Two minus one is one."

7. Repeat the exercise with two more volunteers.

Expand It!

When you think the children are ready, try the exercise with three children and then four.

Square Dance Subtraction

For children who are ready for skip-counting, support the idea of subtracting by twos.

How to Do It

1. Ask the children to stand in two lines that are fairly far apart, facing each other so that each child has a partner.

2. Tell the children they will do a square dance to show going away in twos. This will work best if you can pair with a child or another teacher to show the children what to do.

3. Ask the children to march in toward each other:

   Count four steps in to your partner: one, two, three, four.

   March in place: one, two, three, four.

   Count four steps in: one, two, three, four.

   And four steps back: one, two, three, four.

   Count four steps in: one, two, three, four.

   Hold your partner's hands up high! (Clasp hands to make a bridge)

   Now two go away! First two, go under the bridge! (Walk with your partner under the clasped hands)

   There they go! Two go away. (Sit with your partner as the rest continue)

4. Repeat the steps, encouraging the children to move under the bridge two at a time and then to sit. Continue until everyone is sitting.

Equal Groups

Use this activity to support children's understanding of the concept equal.

How to Do It

1. Ask the children to line up, and lead them in a march around the perimeter of the room.

2. Divide the class into two equal groups and have one half follow you as you march to one side of the room. Then, have the other half follow you marching to the other side of the room. If you have an odd number of students, you will need to be a member of one of the groups.

3. Ask the two groups to turn to face each other, and ask the children, "Are these groups the same size?" Encourage the class to tell you what they think.

4. Ask the children to face a partner in the other group across the room. Give them the following instructions:

   March, march, march, march, high five! (Children march toward the partner and exchange high-fives)

   Freeze!

   March, march, march, march (March back to the spot on the other side of the room)

   Freeze!

   Repeat this three times.

5. Ask the children to sit down with their groups on opposite sides of the room. They should be back in their original spots.

6. Ask the two groups to look at each other, and ask the children, "Are these groups the same size?" Encourage the class to tell you what they think. Ask them how they know. If they need help, encourage them to recognize that they each have a partner. Tell them, "Equal means each group is the same—the same number of children in each group."

7. Help the group on one side of the room count the children in the other group. Then, help the second group count the number of children in the opposite group. Lead the children to understand that there are equal numbers of people in the two groups. The groups are *equal*.

Greater Than, Less Than—Split!

Encourage an understanding of size and comparison.

How to Do It

Depending on the attention spans of the children in your class, this may be a whole-class activity or a smaller group activity. Adjust the size to fit your needs.

1. Line up the children on one side of the classroom in two lines. You stand in the middle of the room. You will need an odd number of people for this activity. If your class has an even number of students, ask another teacher or class helper to join in.

2. Tell the children you will pair them up and ask them to cross the room toward you; then they will split into two groups. One group will go to one corner of the room; the other group will go to the other corner.

3. Start a rhythm by clapping hands or patting thighs to keep the exercise moving, so children tap or clap as they wait in their groups. This makes it feel like teams without winners or losers.

4. Pair up the children. Two by two, each pair starts out together. Call the children by name, and give them an action to do as they move across the room toward you, such as walking, jumping, chugging like a train, or waving their arms in the air. For example, you might say, "Susan and Ethan, jump across the room to me!"

5. When the pair reaches you, say, "Split!" Direct one child to one corner and the other child to another corner. Repeat until there are three children left.

6. Say, "Freeze! Now watch this. This time will be different, and this is the last group to go." This time, have the three children move side by side together toward you.

7. When they get to you, have them stop. Ask the class: "If we put one person in each group every time, then will the groups be the same size?

8. Direct two of the last three children into one group and one of them into the other. Ask the class, "What about now? What happened when we put two children into one group and only one child in the other group?" Help the children understand that one group has more children. It is bigger.

Make a Ball

Help children understand the shape of a circle and how that shape can be moved in space.

How to Do It

1. Ask the children to stand well spaced in a circle, and ask them to pretend to hold an imaginary ball.

2. Give them the following directions:

   Hold your ball (Pretend to hold an imaginary ball in hands)

   Make it bigger (Open arms in ball shape to make the ball bigger)

   Turn it over (Tip arms over in one direction, keeping the ball shape)

   Turn it over the other way (Tip arms over in the other direction, keeping the ball shape)

   Make a big ball in the air (Lift arms overhead, keeping the ball shape)

   And turn yourselves around and around (Turn around and around)

   and around and around! (Continue turning)

   Stop!

   Throw your ball up in the air (Throw the ball high into the air and look up at it)

   And catch it! (Catch it and look at it)

   Again. (Repeat)

   Take your ball anywhere you want to take it in the room! (Carry the ball anywhere in room)

   Bring your ball back to the circle.

   Hold it in your hands.

   And make it smaller and smaller.

   Put it in your pocket!

Expand It!

Pretend to have one imaginary ball and pass it around the circle. Then throw and catch it between the students.

Marching the Shapes

Give children a visual understanding of shapes.

How to Do It

1. Show the children examples of a square, a rectangle, a triangle, and a circle. Talk about each shape: how many sides and corners it has.

2. Tell the children that they are going to march the shapes. Lead them in marching around the room in the pattern of each shape.

3. Square: march five steps, stop, and turn to the right. Repeat four times.

4. Rectangle: march five steps, stop, turn to the right; march seven steps, stop, turn to the right; march five steps, stop, turn to the right; march seven steps, stop, turn to the right.

5. Triangle: walk in straight line across the room; turn to the right; walk straight to a point across the room; turn to the right; walk straight back to the point where you started.

6. Circle: ask the children to hold the hands of two other children. Tell them that this is a circle. Ask them if they see any lines. Lead them to the understanding that it is a round shape and has no lines. Holding hands, walk with the children around in a circle.

Expand It!

Have children take turns leading the class parade in line shapes.

Squiggle and Zip

Explore different ways of moving in lines: straight and squiggly, jumping and hopping.

How to Do It

1. Ask the children to think of ways they can move across the room in lines: jump like a monkey, hop like a bunny, gallop like a horse, swim like an eel.
2. Line up the children on one side of the room. Ask them to experiment:
   - Walk in a straight line
   - Hop in a straight line
   - Gallop in a straight line
   - Walk in a squiggly line
   - Jump in a squiggly line
   - Swim in a squiggly line
   - Zip in a straight line

Expand It!

Have children take turns choosing a way of moving and leading the other children across the room.

Moons and Shooting Stars

Support the children's understanding of linear and circular movements as they experiment with size, distance, and spatial awareness.

How to Do It

1. Ask the children to stand well spaced in the room. Tell them they are going to be moons and shooting stars.
2. Begin by practicing to be moons, slowly spinning in space. Encourage the children to spin and to move in circles. Ask them if they are big moons or little moons.
3. Ask the children to stop and begin turning in the opposite direction.
4. Ask the children to come together to make a big circle and make the circle go around and around all together, first in one direction and then the other.
5. Ask the children to stand in a line on one side of the room and run and leap or zoom across like shooting stars. Ask them if they are big or little. Ask them to stretch out their arms and twinkle and shine with light as they zoom.

Mirror Me

Children work with partners to make shapes with their bodies.

How to Do It

1. Divide the class into two groups and form two lines facing each other.
2. Ask the children in one line to make individual triangle shapes with their bodies; ask the other group to copy them.
3. Ask the children in the second group to make circle shapes with their bodies; ask the first group to copy them.
4. Continue, taking turns asking one group to make a shape and the other to copy the shape.
5. Then have the children spread out around the room and find a partner, or pair them up yourself.
6. Encourage one child to make a shape, such as a square, with her body, and encourage the partner to copy her. Then ask the other child to make a shape and the first child to copy him.

We All Make Shapes

Children work together as they explore making geometric shapes as a group.

How to Do It

1. Teach the children the following rhyme:
   Three makes a triangle,
   Four makes a square,
   We all make a circle if we stand right there!

2. Begin with a triangle. Divide the class into groups of three, and have each group make a triangle with their bodies. They can explore different ways to do this, perhaps by having two children standing and pressing hands against each other while the third child lies down on the floor, or by all three of them lying on the floor.

3. Next, try a square. Divide the class into groups of four. Have each group explore different ways of making a square with their bodies.

4. To make a circle, gather the whole class and join hands. Make a big circle, then move in toward the center to make a smaller circle. Say the rhyme: Three makes a triangle, four makes a square; we all make a circle if we stand right there!

Expand It!

Encourage groups to take turns showing the class how they make a shape.

Action Patterns

Explore pattern sequencing with movement.

How to Do It

1. Teach the children two simple motions, such as clapping and patting thighs. Clap your hands, and then pat your thighs.
2. Tell them that you will make a pattern with your actions and they are to copy you. Begin with an A-B-A-B pattern, such as clap-pat-clap-pat. Do this sitting down, then standing, then walking around.
3. When the children can copy the A-B pattern, change to an A-B-A pattern. For example, clap-pat-clap, first while sitting, then standing, then walking.

Expand It!

Have the children make suggestions to create their own patterns. Encourage each child to take a turn showing an A-B pattern for the class to copy.

Orange, Banana, Orange

Children learn pattern sequencing with words and shapes.

How to Do It

1. Ask the children to stand, spaced widely enough so they can move.
2. Tell them that you will say a word, and they are to make that shape with their bodies. For example, if you say, "Orange," they are to make a round shape with their bodies. They may choose to make a circle with their arms, roll into a ball, or make a circle with their hands. If you say, "Banana," they are to make a long banana shape. They may do this by stretching out and reaching high with their arms, or they may lie on the floor in an arc. Encourage the children to make these shapes in any way that makes sense to them.
3. Start with an A-B-A-B pattern, such as orange-banana-orange-banana. Let the children explore making that pattern.
4. Next, try an A-B-B pattern, such as orange-banana-banana.
5. Continue in this manner, trying different patterns, such as A-A-A-B or B-B-A-A. When the children are comfortable making the patterns, try having fun by changing the shapes quickly to see if the children can follow directions.

Expand It!

Add another element to make an A-B-C pattern, such as orange-banana-grape.

One, Three, One

Explore movement patterns as you support one-to-one correspondence and number sequencing.

How to Do It

1. Teach the children a movement, such as jumping, clapping, or nodding.
2. Tell them that you will call out a number and they are to do the movement that many times. Practice calling out numbers and encouraging the children to do that number of movements.
3. When the children are comfortable with this activity, ask the children to count out loud with you as they do the movements. For example, say, "One, three, one," and ask the children to nod and call out, "One; one, two, three; one," as they nod one time, three times, and one time. Younger children may actually move more or less than the number you call. The important thing is for them to associate counting with the idea of doing an action a certain number of times. Older children can be more precise in the actual number of times they do the action.

One Means Hop; Two Means Wiggle

Children learn patterns as they explore movement.

How to Do It

1. Ask the children to stand with enough room between them so they can move.

2. Pair actions with numbers. For example, tell the children that when you call out the number one, they are to hop. When you call out the number two, they are to wiggle. Practice several times, so the children can remember which action goes with each number. Here, it is the action itself that matters, not how many times children do it when it is called out.

3. Start with an A-B-A pattern, such as 1-2-1, hop, wiggle, hop. Call out, "One, two, one." Encourage the children to hop, wiggle, hop. For younger children, you may have to say, "One, hop! Two, wiggle! One, hop!" Older children will be able to do the movements when they hear the numbers.

4. Try different patterns, such as A-B-B-A and A-A-B-B.

Math Orchestra

Explore action patterns with sounds.

How to Do It

1. Organize the class into three groups, standing in the middle of the room.
2. Give each group a sound and an action to do. First, give the groups of children the sound, such as "beep, beep," or "swoosh, swoosh," or "boom, boom."
3. Then, teach the children the action that goes with the sound, such as bouncing, waving arms in the air, or stomping feet.
4. Next, pair the sound with the action. Let each group practice making their sound and doing their movement. Point to each group when it is their turn to make their sound and action.
5. When the children are comfortable doing their sounds and movements, change the order of how you conduct each group. That way, the class will have to pay attention to where you point.
   Repeat various patterns moving among the three groups.
6. Ask children to remember what sound and action they did in their group. Then, have everyone walk around the room and come back to sit down together in one long line.
7. Point to each child, conducting them, down the line. Ask them to make the same sound and movement they made with their group! The pattern will be random, and a different song will be made by the group each time. Have fun experimenting with different patterns of sound and movement.

Expand It!

Have children take turns being the conductor, pointing to class members to make different patterns.

First, Middle, and Last

This fun activity gives all the children a chance to be first, middle, and last.

How to Do It

1. Ask the children to line up and place one hand on the shoulder of the child in front them.
2. Tell them they will make a choo-choo train and *choo-choo* around the room, making sounds like a train as they go.
3. Tell them that the child in the front is *first*. The child at the back of the line is *last,* and the children in between are in the *middle*.
4. Let the train move around the room; then say, "Freeze." Ask the first child to move to the last position, and ask the child who is second in line to be *first*. Ask the children in between to tell where they are—the *middle*!
5. Continue, letting each child take a turn being first and last. The children in between are in the middle.

Bluebird, Won't You Come and Fly with Me?

Support learning of the concepts of high and low, in and out.

How to Do It

1. Teach the children the following song (a variation on the traditional "Bluebird, Bluebird through My Window"):

   Bluebird, bluebird at my window
   Bluebird, bluebird at my window
   Bluebird, bluebird on my doorstep
   Won't you come and fly with me?

2. Ask the children to sit in a circle or in a long line, spaced far enough apart that a person may walk between them.

3. One at a time or in pairs, ask the children to stand tall on their tiptoes with arms flapping like wings and to move around the circle or weave through the circle while the rest of the children sing along with the song.

   - Ask the children to pretend to fly high in the sky and low toward the ground.
   - Ask the children to pretend to fly in and out of the windows by weaving in and out of the line.

Expand It!

Use the exercise to teach other concepts such as near and far or together and apart.

Brown Bear, Move like This!

This fun variation of the game Red Rover teaches listening skills and patterns of movement.

How to Do It

1. Tell children they will play a game called Brown Bear. They will be the bears. You will call out, "Brown bear, brown bear, move like this over there!" Then you will give them three motions to do as they cross the room.

2. Ask the children to line up near the wall. Divide them into three groups.

3. You stand on the other side of the room and call out to the first group, "Brown bear, brown bear, move like this over there: zigzag, jump, and bear walk."

4. Encourage the children to cross the room, one at a time, with the motions you gave them.

5. For the second group, say, "Brown bear, brown bear, move like this over there: leap, walk, and kick big legs."

6. Encourage each child to move across the room in the three motions you listed. Other suggestions for movements:
   - crouch, jump, and balance on one foot
   - turn, jump, and wiggle
   - hop, spin, and clap
   - gallop, walk, and clap

7. Continue the game, giving the three groups more movements to do as they cross back to the other side of the room.

Expand It!

Have children take turns being the caller and inventing a pattern of movements to call out.

Counting Obstacle Course

Reinforce gross motor skills, eye-hand coordination, and spatial awareness while building pattern recognition and counting skills.

How to Do It

1. Create an obstacle course in the classroom or outside with items such as small- and medium-sized mats, flat rubber dots, wedges, tape lines, hula-hoops, cones or buckets, scarves, and tunnels.

2. At each station, place a sign with a numeral on it. The number at each station will represent the number of times an action should be performed and the order in which to do the stations. For younger children, create a three-station course. Older children will be able to do a five-station course or more.

3. The following are suggestions for actions to perform at each station:

   - Small-sized mats—leap over, hop onto, twirl or spin on, "magic spot" (freestyle movement/dance)
   - Medium-sized mats—roll across, crawl over, march across, tiptoe across, walk with wide legs
   - Flat rubber dots—hop along, use as stepping stones, jump wide and narrow, twirl or spin on
   - Hula-hoops—jump into, hula with, wiggle in
   - Tape line—balance along, walk sideways on (step together), hop along on one foot
   - Wedge—walk up and leap off, crawl up, roll down, balance on
   - Cones—weave around, walk between, crawl or slither between
   - Scarves—grab and move to another bucket, hold and twirl, leap with

   You may also choose to use stations indoors with no props:

   - Area rug—hop onto, leap over, "magic spot" (freestyle movement/dance)
   - Hanging mobile—jump straight up, spin or twirl underneath
   - Alphabet wall—touch toes, jump feet open and closed, wiggle, gallop past
   - Front door—take a bow, low kicks, pump arms, march in circle
   - Windows—wiggle, walk sideways on (step together)
   - Child's own seat—hop on one foot
   - Bare floor—tap dance, fast feet
   - Carpeted floor—slow motion run, leap, crawl or slither on belly, log roll

Tables—walk or run around, create a pathway to weave through

4. Demonstrate the course to the children two or three times before they begin. For the second and third demonstrations, have them call out with you the number of the station and what action is required, verbalizing their understanding of the obstacle course.

5. Let the children go through the obstacle course one at a time, making sure to allow plenty of lead time before the next child in line begins.

Expand It!

Encourage the children to do problem solving by creating their own three-station obstacle courses.

Resources

Block, Betty. 2001. "Literacy through Movement: An Organizational Approach."
Journal of Physical Education, Recreation & Dance 72(1): 39–48.

Bransford, John, Ann Brown, and Rodney Cocking, eds. 2000. *How People Learn: Brain, Mind, Experience, and School.* 2nd ed. Washington, DC: National Academy Press.

Brownell, Kelly, and Katherine Horgen. 2004. *Food Fight: The Inside Story of the Food Industry, America's Obesity Crisis, and What We Can Do about It.* New York: McGraw-Hill.

Carlson, Frances M. 2011. *Big Body Play.* Washington, DC: National Association for the Education of Young Children.

Cohen, Bonnie B. 2008. *Sensing, Feeling, and Action.* 2nd ed. Northampton, MA: Contact Editions.

Deiner, Penny L., and Wei Qui. 2007. "Embedding Physical Activity and Nutrition in Early Care and Educational Programs." *Zero to Three* (28)1: 13–18.

Elliot, Eloise, and Steve Sanders. 2002. "Children and Physical Activity: The Importance of Movement and Physical Activity." PBS Teachers.
http://www.pbs.org/teachers/earlychildhood/articles/physical.html.

Gerber, F. Joyce. 2008. *Teaching with Heart.* Bridgeport, CT: Teaching with Heart LLC Publications.

Hannaford, Carla. 2005. *Smart Moves: Why Learning Is Not All in Your Head.* 2nd ed. Arlington, VA: Great Ocean.

National Association for Sports and Physical Education. 2009. *Active Start: A Statement of Physical Activity Guidelines for Children from Birth to Age 5.* 2nd ed. Reston, VA: NASPE.

Neuman, Susan, Carol Copple, and Sue Bredekamp. 2000. *Learning to Read and Write: Developmentally Appropriate Practices for Young Children.* Washington, DC: National Association for the Education of Young Children.

Olds, Anita. 1994. "From Cartwheels to Caterpillars: Children's Need to Move Indoors and Out." *Building Opportunities for Gross Motor Development* (97): 32–36.

Pica, Rae. 2007. *Jump into Literacy: Active Learning for Preschool Children.* Beltsville, MD: Gryphon House.

Pica, Rae. 2008. *Jump into Math: Active Learning for Preschool Children.* Beltsville, MD: Gryphon House.

Pica, Rae. 2009. *Jump into Science: Active Learning for Preschool Children.* Beltsville, MD: Gryphon House.

Pica, Rae. 2006. *Moving and Learning Across the Curriculum*. 2nd ed. Independence, KY: Wadsworth.

Puhl, Rebecca. 2011. "Weight Stigmatization toward Youth: A Significant Problem in Need of Societal Solutions." *Childhood Obesity* 7(5): 359–63.

Ratey, John. 2008. *Spark: The Revolutionary New Science of Exercise and the Brain*. New York: Little, Brown.

Singer, Dorothy, and Jerome Singer. 2005. *Imagination and Play in the Electronic Age*. Cambridge, MA: Harvard University Press.

Timmons, Brian, Patti-Jean Naylor, and Karin Pfeiffer. 2007. "Physical Activity for Preschool Children—How Much and How?" *Applied Physiology, Nutrition, and Metabolism* 32(S2E): S122–S134.

Wardle, Francis. n.d. "Play as Curriculum." *Early Childhood News*. http://www.earlychildhoodnews.com/earlychildhood/article_view.aspx?ArticleID=127.

Willis, Judy. 2008. *How Your Child Learns Best: Brain-Friendly Strategies You Can Use to Ignite Your Child's Learning and Increase School Success*. Naperville, IL: Sourcebooks.

Yale Rudd Center for Food Policy and Obesity. www.yaleruddcenter.org.

Index